Gloucester Road Women's Institute presents

The Gloucester Road
Cookbook

A collection of recipes by the independent traders
of Gloucester Road and members of Gloucester Rd WI

Published by Gloucester Road WI

www.GloucesterRdWI.tumblr.com
GloucesterRdWI@yahoo.com

Gloucester Road WI
Office 34, New House
67-68 Hatton Garden
London EC1N 8JY

ISBN 978-0-9926453-0-4

British Library Cataloguing in Publication Data
A CIP catalogue record for this book is available from the British Library

All design, illustrations and photography (unless stated) © India Rabey. Printed by Berforts Group Ltd on responsibly sourced paper.

The Gloucester Road
Cookbook

A collection of recipes by the independent traders
of Gloucester Road and members of Gloucester Rd WI

Created exclusively using
the skills and talents of
Gloucester Rd WI members

Sponsored by:

Supporting:

In the Community For the Community

Bishopston Matters

SURVIVE
WORKING TOWARDS
FREEDOM FROM
DOMESTIC ABUSE

Foreword

Xanthe Clay: author, chef, writer and local food hero.

Walking down the Gloucester Road makes me proud to live in Bristol. The range of shops, from the proper family butchers to the specialist home brewing shop, the greengrocer, the Italian deli, the independent jewellers, the Vietnamese supermarket and the proper bakers, is the British high street at its finest.

It's worth supporting – and that means using it. Raymond Blanc puts it most pithily. When you buy an apple, you don't just choose whether it is imported, or organic, or a heritage variety, he told me (I'm paraphrasing), you choose whether you want a post office in your village or your local shops to survive. Up to you.

That's reason enough. But in fact, those of us who shop on the Gloucester Road do so just because we love it. We love the shops and the quality of what we can buy there – at great prices too, although the multiples would love you to believe that bargains only exist in a supermarket. And we love the shopkeepers, the service and the experience of the community.

Now, another reason to love the Gloucester Road, is this book of dishes collected from locals and businesses. The best recipes are always the ones that come not from celebrity chefs but from real people, tried and tested in their own homes – and that is exactly what you have here. Not only that – but you might even bump into the author of the recipe you are cooking when you go shopping for ingredients, so you can ask for advice right from the expert, tell them how you got on, let them know how you made the dish your own.

It's a book for enjoying, sharing and talking about, just like Gloucester Road itself. Let the cooking begin!

Xanthe

Contents

Key to recipes

V Vegetarian dish

Vg Vegan dish

D Dairy-free

Wine matching
p172

Steaming rice
p176

Gloucester Road

Gloucester Road is a unique road, which meanders through the communities of Bishopston, St Andrews and Horfield and contains a wide range of shops, cafes, pubs and restaurants. It is the heart of our community and has something for everyone.

Trading on Gloucester Road started in the late 1800s to meet the needs of local people as homes were being built in the area. It has evolved today into a high street with a large proportion of independent businesses and is locally renowned as the longest independent high street in the United Kingdom.

The road has changed in the last 20 years with plenty of new shops appearing amongst old favourites and the growth of independently run coffee shops, bars and restaurants. There has been a tremendous increase in specialist shops as well as a strong presence of high street staples such as butchers, fishmongers, bakeries and greengrocers which sadly have become a dying breed in some other parts of the city.

It is not hard to see why Gloucester Road is a special place for the local community. In a time when we often hear of the decline of the high street, it is thriving. You really can buy everything you need on

Gloucester Road without visiting the large retail outlets and there is a huge amount of affection and loyalty for the area. People enjoy shopping and spending their money there; not only due to the variety of shops, but also because of the personal service from shopkeepers who know their customers and appreciate their loyalty.

As a group of women who live locally, we hope this book reflects our support for our high street.

Gloucester Road, circa 1912. With Pearce's on the far right.
©Bygone Bristol. www.bygonebristol.co.uk

Live Local

Many of our contributing traders accept payment by Bristol Pound, our city's very own currency. If a business accepts Bristol Pound as payment, you'll find this handy logo £ at the bottom of their page.

BRISTOL POUND
OUR CITY. OUR MONEY.

Map

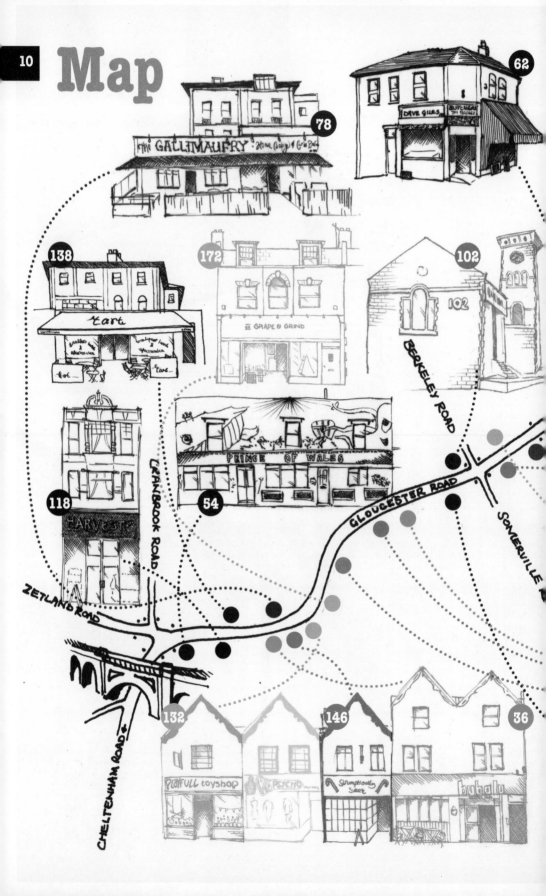

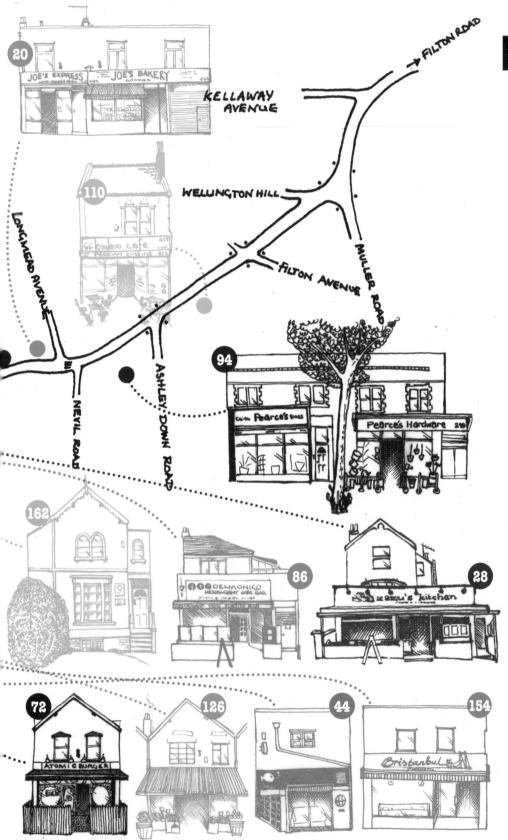

Not to scale. Illustrations © India Rabey.

Gloucester Road, taken July 1913. Now 102 Cookery School on left (p102) and Gardner's Patch on right (p126).

©Bygone Bristol. www.bygonebristol.co.uk

Opposite: Some of the many independent retailers that Gloucester Road is famous for.

Background to the book

The Women's Instititute is synonymous with cooking and there are stereotypes of members whipping up a showstopper in their sleep and practicing jam-making as something to do of a Friday evening. As times change and the average age of a WI member decreases, more of our members work full-time, leading to the rise of the post-7pm monthly meeting and the need for nutritious, easy to prepare dishes that anyone can prepare and family and friends will also love.

Being based in an area like Gloucester Road, we, like most of the community that surrounds us, enjoy the simple things in life; buying our fruit and veg from the greengrocer rather than the supermarket and purchasing our meat from a butcher who can tell us its origin. Living around a thriving high street, we have adopted the independent shopping spirit and want to support the traders that we appreciate so much.

When Katie, our project leader, came up with the idea of a Gloucester Road cookbook, she wanted to celebrate the diversity and the wide range of foods that can be picked up along Gloucester Road – using the book to illustrate the incredibly varied dishes that can be prepared with ingredients bought on our doorsteps.

By getting local traders involved, we hope to celebrate their successful businesses by showcasing their favourite recipes, whether they are dishes that they serve in their restaurants or cafes, or old favourites that represent them. Our lovely WI members have also let us into their top secret recipes too, making for a cookbook packed with great ideas and recipes from around the world, with some steeped in memories, having come through several generations.

Sections

The book is divided into courses so that whether you're looking for a small snack, ideas for entertaining or the perfect pudding, you can flick straight to the relevant part of the book. And with tips on the difficulty rating, preparation and cooking times to hand at the bottom of each recipe too, you'll know in advance what you're getting yourself into! Vegetarian, vegan and dairy-free recipes will also be marked in the key to the top right of each recipe.

The Project

Putting our heads together at the end of 2012, we pulled together a team of Gloucester Rd WI members. Comprising a project manager or two, a designer and photographer, a writer, a chef, a publisher, some financial whizzes and several food enthusiasts, we began work in earnest, chatting to businesses to drum up support and gather recipes. *Bishopston Matters*, a local community magazine delivered to 10,500 homes per quarter around Bishopston, St Andrews, Horfield and Ashley Down, became our premium sponsor and have even contributed a recipe.

With the help of our sponsors and the traders who have been involved in the book, we have managed to raise the majority of the printing costs. The remainder was raised by two fantastic fundraising events: our Tea Party in April 2013 and a Spring Fayre in June. A mountain of cake was kindly donated and then devoured for each event, and we raised much more for the project than we could have ever hoped. Proceeds from the sale of the book will be donated to Survive, a charity chosen by Gloucester Rd WI as well as going towards future community WI projects.

The book finally came together in July 2013 and we sent it off to print in August. Having taken a lot of hard work to get here, we are enormously proud of what we've achieved. We hope that all of you – locals, traders or strangers who have simply heard of our wonderful Gloucester Road through someone you know – love the final product as much as we do.

St. Michael and All Angels Church, GRWI's current monthly meeting place.

The Women's Institute

After beginning in Canada in 1897, the Women's Institute came to British shores in 1915. Started as a way to encourage countrywomen to get involved with growing and preserving food to increase the supply of food to Britain during World War I, groups multiplied quickly until by the end of the decade, Britain had 1405 WIs across the country.

Numbers have increased even more since then, dipping through the 80s and 90s but rising again now due to the resurgence in a traditional way of living so often associated with the WI.

The WI's return to form has been attributed to many things including the increase in popularity of growing your own food, craft, and cooking, and that it has become a new way for women to socialise and enjoy themselves. Associations with 'Jam and Jerusalem' and *Calendar Girls* are slowly fading and in many parts of the UK, a new, more modern take on the traditional values held by the WI are making waves.

The WI is described as providing women with educational opportunities, a chance to build new skills, to take part in a range of activities and to campaign on issues that matter to them. Every year, resolutions are passed on issues voted on at the AGM. With issues such as the 'Keep Britain Tidy' campaign and the closure of libraries having been previous concerns, 2013's resolution is to protect our high streets. This book goes hand in hand with what the WI aim to do this year through this resolution.

The WI has come full circle since it began 100 years ago, becoming more relevant today in every respect; through its resolutions, activities held at their educational facility, Denman College, and most importantly, through its members. Women may not always join the WI for the same reasons these days but whether it be making friends in a new city, learning interesting skills, sharing their knowledge and insight, or simply to have a night out

with the girls once a month, women continue to join. This means that the Women's Institute will continue to reign supreme.

Gloucester Rd WI

Gloucester Rd WI was started by India Rabey and a small group of friends in November 2011 after she moved to the area and discovered there was no local WI meeting in the evenings.

We now have 100 members and meet on the third Tuesday of every month at St Michael and All Angels Church Hall. With a varied and eclectic programme of meetings throughout the year, from the traditional bake off, to talks of polar exploration and lots of extra clubs to get involved in, the WI has something for every woman.

GloucesterRdWI.tumblr.com
TheWI.org.uk

SURVIVE

WORKING TOWARDS FREEDOM FROM DOMESTIC ABUSE

The charity

Survive is an innovative local charity working towards freedom from domestic abuse for women and children in Bristol and South Gloucestershire. We offer practical and emotional support, accommodation, information and education for women, children and young people who are experiencing or have experienced domestic violence and abuse. Last year we worked with over 600 women and children.

Research shows that domestic violence is most commonly experienced by women; up to 90% of recorded abuse is perpetrated by men towards women but domestic abuse can and does happen to anyone, irrespective of gender, age, social class, religion or sexual orientation.

Survive are delighted to have been chosen by Gloucester Rd WI to benefit from the sale of this cookbook and I thank you on behalf of Survive, and all the women and children whose lives this generous donation will have an impact on.

"OMG! I married the persuader, what an insight. I now understand how he has affected my life. Without this group I would still be living with my children in an abusive environment. I need this group, the support is second to none, and no other establishment has helped keep me and my family safe."

Former Survive group participant.

The money will go towards running our Freedom Programme. The Freedom Programme is our group work programme for women who have experienced domestic abuse. It helps them recover from their experiences, recognise potential future abusers and recognise the effects of domestic abuse on children. It also supports them to help each other and form a network of support. Isolation often forms a central part of domestic abuse.

The Freedom Programme makes a real difference to the lives of women and children who have experienced abuse.

Gillian Carson,
Sustainability Manager,
Survive

www.survivedv.org.uk

Light bites

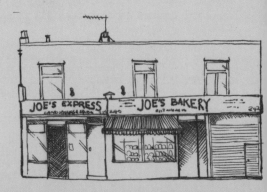

Recipe by **Emma Davis**

Emma is a Bishopston mum of
two little boys aged two and four.

UNDER 30 MINS

High iron muesli & granola

V Vg D

I created this muesli recipe to help increase my iron levels after the birth of my two boys. After taking supplements for a while I started to look for more natural ways to boost the iron in my diet. The addition of fresh berries helps you to maximise the iron from the dried fruit, nuts, and seeds as vitamin C increases absorption of iron from plant sources.

Basic muesli recipe

500g jumbo oats
150g pumpkin seeds
200g cashew nuts
150g dried apricots, chopped

To make granola

75g butter
125g light brown sugar
175g honey, maple syrup or golden syrup

TOP TIP

You can refresh the granola in the oven if it loses its crunch.

Method

For the muesli: Mix all of the ingredients together and serve with a handful of fresh berries and milk and/or natural yoghurt and honey.

For the granola: Preheat oven to 180°C.

Add the butter, sugar and honey to a saucepan. Heat gently over a low heat until the butter has melted and the sugar has dissolved. Leave to cool slightly then stir into the dry muesli ingredients. Add any combination of other ingredients if required.

Pour the mixture into a large, lined roasting tray. Leave some air gaps, do not press down into tin. Bake for 10-15 minutes until golden and crisp, stirring in the middle of cooking to allow air to circulate. This will need to be done in two or three batches.

Leave to cool and give the granola a good stir to break up. Serve as before or carry around to nibble as a high energy snack.

Difficulty: ●○○○○
Preparation time: 10 min (muesli) and 10 min (granola)
Cooking time: 45 mins (granola)

Serving: Makes approximately 15 servings

Storage: Store in an airtight container at room temperature. This should keep fresh and crunchy for two weeks.

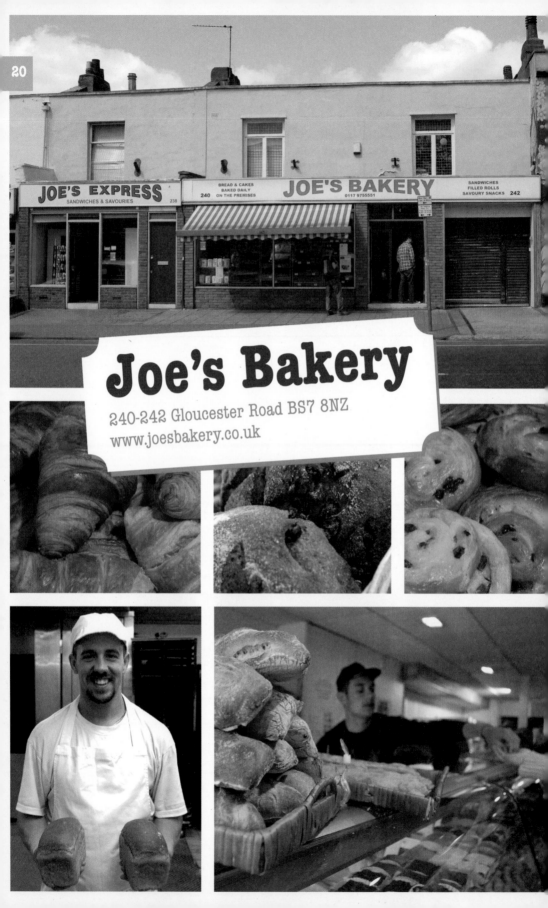

Joe's Bakery

240-242 Gloucester Road BS7 8NZ
www.joesbakery.co.uk

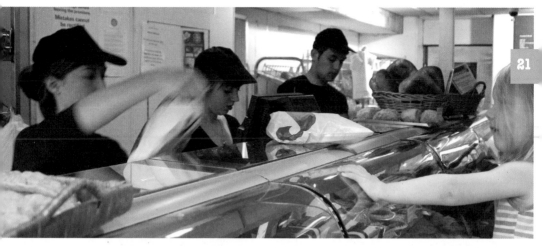

Joe's Bakery has been run by Martin and Jane Hunt since 1990 when they moved to Gloucester Road from a small bakery in Brislington. They couldn't wait to start trading on Gloucester Road because of its locality and reputation; did you know there has been a bakery on the site since the late 1800s?

Specialising in a fabulous range of British and continental breads as well as a huge selection of cakes, pastries and doughnuts, Joe's Bakery attracts customers from all over the city. And the couple even provide the locals with a quick lunchtime solution at Joe's Express next door where they do a roaring trade in pasties, pies and ready made sandwiches and rolls.

"We love the Gloucester Road for its great, lifelong memories, its vibrancy, its great mix of shops and the wonderful support we get from local residents," says Jane.

Two small brown loaves

Ⓥ

An increasingly popular loaf at Joe's Bakery, this recipe was one of several used for the 'National Loaf' during World War II. It is considered by nutritionists to be the ideal balance of dietary fibre and starch.

Ingredients

250g strong white flour

250g strong wholemeal flour

8g butter

7g fresh yeast

8g fine sea salt

315g water

To make it a vegan friendly and dairy-free loaf, simply swap butter with vegetable shortening or all vegetable margarine.

Method

Place the flour and butter in a large mixing bowl. Place the yeast in one side of the bowl and the salt in the other so that they don't initially come into direct contact with each other.

Make a well in the centre, add the water and mix into the flour using a spatula or your fingertips. Squash the dough into the bottom of the bowl and squeeze together with your fingertips. Continue until there is little or no loose, dry flour in the bowl.

Empty the dough onto a lightly-floured work surface. Using one hand to hold the dough in place, push and stretch the dough away from your body with the heel of the other hand. Curl the flattened dough back into a log shape and, with the 'log' pointing away from you, continue kneading until the dough is smooth and stretchy. This should take around 10 minutes.

Leave the dough in a bowl, covered with a clean tea towel or a plastic bag, in a warm place for 1-2 hours until the dough has at least doubled in size.

Divide the dough into two even pieces and mould into the shape of your two loaf tins. Lightly oil the tins (or trays) and put the dough into them. Leave the dough, covered, in a warm place for 40-50 minutes until an indent is left when it is lightly pressed – this means the loaf is ready to bake. Whilst the dough is proving, preheat the oven to 230°C. When the loaves are ready to bake, lightly dust each with wholemeal flour.

Bake for 20-22 minutes. When ready, the loaves should sound hollow when the bottom is tapped. Cool before eating.

Difficulty: ●●○○○
Preparation time: 20 mins plus 2-3 hours proving time
Cooking time: 25 mins

Serving: Approximately 12 slices per loaf

Storage: Keep in a bread bin or paper bag in a cupboard for three days. Suitable for freezing, use within one month.

Recipe by **Rosa Blanch**

Rosa works for the sustainable transport charity, Sustrans, and lives just off the Gloucester Road.

UNDER 30 MINS

Saturday brunch

This is simple, quick and regularly provides fuel for my late Saturday morning potter down the Gloucester Road. I developed a love for poached eggs while visiting friends in Canada; they would poach eggs every day for breakfast after they had returned from early morning rowing training.

Ingredients

3 rashers of bacon

An egg

50ml white wine vinegar

Butter

A bagel

½ avocado, peeled, de-stoned and thinly sliced

Salt and pepper

Method

Place the bacon under a preheated grill and turn occasionally until cooked to your liking, or fry in a dry frying pan.

Meanwhile, break the egg into a mug. Bring a large pan of water to the boil, enough to completely cover the egg. Add the white wine vinegar to the boiling water and stir to create a vortex. Reduce the heat then place the egg into the middle of the vortex in the water. Simmer for 3 minutes whilst toasting the bagels.

When ready, remove the egg from the pan using a slotted spoon and leave to drain on a wooden board.

Butter the bagel, add avocado slices and bacon, placing the poached egg on top.

Season and eat!

Difficulty: ● ● ○ ○ ○
Preparation time: 5 mins
Cooking time: 20 mins

Serving: 1

Storage: Best eaten fresh.

Recipe by **Sarah Miller**

Sarah lives in St Andrews and was once Easyjet's 150 millionth customer, winning free flights for a year!

UNDER 30 MINS

Savoury muffins

This is a really flexible recipe for you to mix and match flavours. You could substitute the carrot for courgette or even beetroot. Cooked smoked streaky bacon or cubed pancetta is also a good addition. The buttermilk combined with the carrot makes them really light and moist and they are great for breakfast.

Ingredients

1 tbsp olive oil

1 red onion, finely chopped

1 red chilli, finely chopped

250g wholemeal self raising flour

2 tsp baking powder

½ tsp bicarbonate of soda

¼ tsp salt

2 eggs

80g unsalted butter, melted and cooled

200ml buttermilk

1 carrot, grated

Couple of handfuls of strong cheddar, grated

Method

Preheat oven to 200°C and fill a muffin tin with 12 paper muffin cases.

Heat the oil in a pan and gently fry the onion and chilli over a medium heat until softened but not browned. Set aside to cool.

Mix together the flour, baking powder, bicarbonate of soda and salt in a large bowl. Whisk the eggs, butter and buttermilk in a jug and add to the flour mixture. Stir with a spatula until just mixed then fold in the carrot, cheese and the sautéed onion and chilli mixture. The mixture should be fairly thick and gloopy but add more buttermilk if you think it needs thinning slightly.

Spoon the mixture into the cases, top with more cheese if you wish and bake for around 18 minutes until the tops of the muffins spring back when pressed.

TOP TIP

If using bacon or pancetta in your muffins, don't add salt.

Difficulty: ●●○○○
Preparation time: 10 mins
Cooking time: 18 mins

Serving: Makes 12 muffins

Storage: Store in an airtight container and eat within three days.

Zazu's Kitchen

225 Gloucester Road BS7 8NR

www.zazuskitchen.co.uk

When Toby Bywater and his business partner James Savage opened the doors to **Zazu's Kitchen** on May 17th 2012, their dream of providing affordable new British cuisine to the hungry masses of Gloucester Road was made a reality.

After a short stop in Stokes Croft and a Clifton pop-up, the pair chose number 225 for its sun-trap tendencies, convenient roadside parking and infinite charm. "Gloucester Road is great. I love the same thing that everyone loves about it. You walk from one end to the other and there is something for absolutely everyone," marvels Toby.

Offering a wonderful range of locally sourced seasonal dishes with produce from the likes of Buxton Butchers, Wing Of St Mawes and La Chasse, Toby also uses fellow cookbook contributors Dave Giles Meats and Joe's Bakery for his meat and bread and points out that the first thing in mind when he chooses suppliers is freshness.

With a carefully written, ever-changing menu taking elements from the backgrounds of their French, Italian and British chefs, Zazu's offer fantastic value for money (you can eat breakfast, lunch and dinner here for under £20) and a beautiful place to eat, whatever the occasion.

Hay-smoked mackerel & gooseberry compôte

This is a simple, but delicious light lunch from Zazu's Kitchen that shows how easy it can be to smoke your own food at home. The tang of the gooseberry compôte complements the oily mackerel brilliantly. Serve with a parsley and shallot salad on sourdough toast.

Ingredients

400g gooseberries, topped and tailed

25g caster sugar

Squeeze of lemon juice

8 fillets of mackerel, pin bones removed

Salt and pepper

1 bunch of flat leaf parsley

2 large banana shallots

Capers

Sourdough loaf

Equipment

For the smoking process, you will need a wire rack that will balance on top of, or fit inside a suitable metal container such as a deep saucepan, roasting tray or old biscuit tin; some hay (easy and cheap to get from your local pet shop) and a roll of tin foil.

Make sure your kitchen is well ventilated whilst smoking the fish.

Method

Place the gooseberries in a saucepan with the sugar and a tablespoon of water. Cook over a low heat for around five minutes until the gooseberries are soft and then check for sweetness, adding a touch more sugar if needed, although a bit of tartness is desirable. If it is slightly too sweet then a good squeeze of lemon juice will help to balance this out. Set aside to cool.

Season the mackerel fillets generously with salt and pepper and set aside for 5 minutes. Grease the wire rack to prevent the fish from sticking, then place the fillets skin side down onto it. Preheat oven to 180°C.

Pack a layer of hay down firmly into the base of your chosen smoking vessel and place on top of a hob over a high heat. Once smoke begins to appear from the hay, place the wire rack on top of the pan/tin and leave for a few seconds to make sure that the hay is smouldering sufficiently (though you don't want it to actually catch fire).

Cover the wire rack and pan with tin foil, leaving a small opening in one corner to allow air in. Smoke on the hob over a medium heat for 4-5 minutes before transferring the whole thing to the oven for a further few minutes to finish cooking. The mackerel should be a pale golden colour and be just cooked through.

To prepare the parsley and shallot salad, which should be done just before serving, pick the parsley, removing the larger stalks. Peel, top and tail the shallots before slicing lengthways as thinly as possible. Mix together the shallots, parsley and a small handful of capers and dress with a simple dressing (p174).

Toast the sourdough and serve buttered with the mackerel, salad and gooseberry compôte.

TOP TIP

Rhubarb, quince and redcurrant will work just as well with this recipe if gooseberries aren't in season.

Difficulty: ●●●○○
Preparation time: 20 mins
Cooking time: 30 mins

Serving: 4

Storage: Keep covered in fridge and eat within three days.

Recipe by
Michaela Parker
Our very own writer who lives in
Horfield with her partner, Jonny.

Grandma's pea and ham soup

As a child, this was something we had for tea regularly after school at Grandma's house. She'd serve it atop homemade chips and my brother, sister and I all loved it. It's cheap to make so it carried me through uni days and continues to be one of my favourites for a cold Autumn day.

For the ham

1 unsmoked, uncooked ham hock/shank
1 onion, sliced
1 carrot, chopped
1 stick of celery, chopped
1 bay leaf

For the soup

500g dried marrowfat peas
1 ham shank/hock as prepared above or bought
1 onion, sliced
1-2 carrots, chopped finely
Black pepper
Approximately 1½ litres cold water

Method

Prepare the peas by soaking them overnight (or follow the instructions on the packet).

To cook the ham (which can also be done the night before if required), place it in a large pan with the other ingredients, cover with water and cook over a medium heat for 2-3 hours until tender.

To make the soup, remove the ham from the shank, trim the fat and roughly chop the meat. If the ham you use has no bone, simply chop the meat into pieces.

Place the meat into a large pan with the onion and carrot. Cover with the cold water and season well with black pepper. Bring to the boil and simmer for 15 minutes.

Rinse the peas. Add them to pan and top up the water to cover all the ingredients. Bring back to the boil and allow to simmer for around 40 minutes, until the peas are cooked and soup is thick and mushy.

Serve with hand cut chips for a dinner option or doorstep bread and butter for lunch.

TOP TIP

Use the stock created by cooking the ham as a replacement for the water in the recipe.

Difficulty: ●○○○○
Preparation time: 20 mins plus ham cooking/soaking time
Cooking time: 1 hour

Serving: 6

Storage: Keep covered in fridge and use within three days. Suitable for freezing. Reheat thoroughly.

Recipe by **Katie Mack**

Katie has been collecting moving pens
for over 25 years and has over 400!

Coconut dahl soup

So yummy, almost everyone who ever tries this soup asks for the recipe.

Ingredients

1 tbsp olive oil

2 cloves of garlic, crushed

1 medium onion, finely chopped

½ tsp turmeric

1 tsp garam masala

¼ tsp chilli powder

1 tsp ground cumin

400g tin of chopped tomatoes

150g red lentils

2 tsp lemon juice

600ml vegetable stock

400g tin of reduced fat coconut milk

A small bunch of coriander, chopped

Method

Heat the oil in a large saucepan and sauté the garlic and onion for 2-3 mins. Add the turmeric, garam masala, chilli powder and cumin and cook for a further 30 seconds or so, allowing the flavours to infuse.

Stir in the tomatoes, red lentils, lemon juice, stock and coconut milk and bring to the boil.

Reduce the heat and simmer, uncovered, for 25-30 mins until the lentils are tender.

Remove from the heat, season to taste and stir in the coriander.

Serve with naan bread.

For a thicker dahl as opposed to soup, use an extra 50g of lentils.

Difficulty: ●○○○○
Preparation time: 5 mins
Cooking time: 35-40 mins

Serving: 6

Storage: Keep covered in fridge and use within three days. Suitable for freezing. Reheat thoroughly.

Bubalu

79/81 Gloucester Road BS7 8AS

www.bubalu.co.uk

FRESH FRUIT
JUICES &
SMOOTHIES

GOURMET
COFFEE

BREAKFAST
CREPES
SALADS
WRAPS
SOUP
NOODLES

As Bristol's one and only fitness cafe, Mike Bowen set up **Bubalu** in 2011 with an aim. As well as providing people with a unique range of fitness classes using the best trainers in the South West, he wants to teach the attendees the importance of post-workout nutrition, steering people away from the common notion that a visit to the gym should be followed by a visit to the vending machine in many reception areas. "It's not about persecuting people because they eat crisps or chocolate," he says. "It's about saying, 'This is how your body works, if you consume more than you expend, you'll put on weight. It's as simple as that!"

A personal trainer for ten years, Mike runs classes as well as running the cafe which offers a range of delicious and nutritious snacks including crepes, wraps and soups as well as juices, smoothies and frozen yoghurts. With coffee from Clifton Coffee Company and a wide range of teas on offer too, customers are also welcome to the spacious cafe to get their daily caffeine fix.

Whether it's a session in their dedicated spin studio, or a Zumba, kettlebells, pilates or kickboxing class, Bubalu inject fun into everything they do. So if you're giving a new class a go, trying a delicious salad or having a coffee with friends, Bubalu is the perfect place to while away an afternoon.

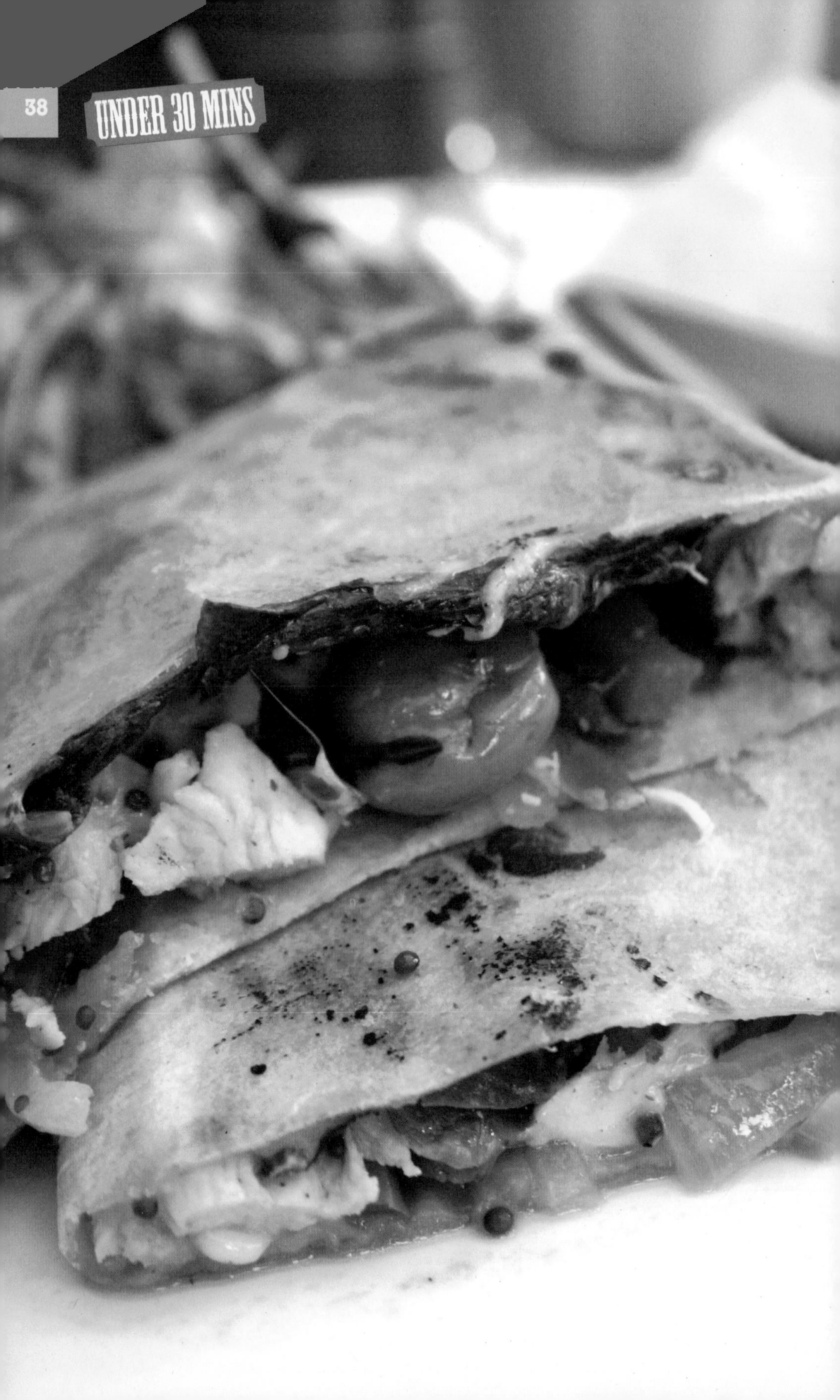

Bubalu B Wrap

Bubalu's signature wrap packs a punch with plenty of vegetables and some great spicy flavours. This recipe can be made at home without a panini press, as is used in the café.

Ingredients

1 tbsp olive oil

1 chicken breast, cut into small chunks and seasoned

1 red or yellow pepper, sliced

1 red onion, finely sliced

½ tsp chilli flakes

1 clove of garlic, finely chopped

Handful of grated hard mozzarella

2 large flour tortillas (make your own, see p46)

15 pitted olives, black or green

Handful of spinach

A few basil leaves crushed and finely sliced so the flavour comes through

1 tbsp honey and 1tbsp wholegrain mustard mixed to make a dressing

Method

Preheat oven to 180°C.

In a frying pan, heat the oil and fry the seasoned chicken until browned on all sides – about two minutes on a high heat. Reduce the heat to medium and add the sliced peppers, onion and chilli flakes, frying for a further three minutes until everything is soft. Remove from the heat and add the garlic so it softens in the heat of the mixture, but does not burn.

Sprinkle a thin layer of mozzarella on the tortillas, then spoon the mixture evenly out into the tortillas and add the olives, spinach and basil.

Finally, drizzle the honey and mustard dressing over the filling, roll it all up, tucking in the sides like a burrito and wrap individually in baking paper/foil to make a tight parcel. Place on the top shelf of the oven for 8 minutes.

Remove from the oven and take paper away. Serve with a side salad with a balsamic dressing (p174).

Difficulty: ●●○○○
Preparation time: 10 mins
Cooking time: 15 mins

Serving: 2

Storage: Best eaten fresh.

Three dips

Inspired by **Fiona Reid**

Fiona is originally from Glasgow
but has lived in Bristol for 25 years.

Shop-bought houmous is great, but you can make your own far cheaper and with the ability to add more or less of each ingredient to suit your tastebuds, budget, dietary requirements and cupboard ingredients.

V

Houmous

400g tin chickpeas, drained and rinsed

Juice of half a lemon

1 clove of garlic, peeled and chopped

1-2 tbsp extra virgin olive oil

1-2 heaped tsp light tahini

Salt and pepper, to taste

2 tbsp cold water

½ tsp ground cumin

½ tsp ground coriander

½ tsp paprika

Method

Tip all the ingredients into a blender and blitz until smooth, scraping down the sides of the blender at short intervals. If the mixture looks too dry, add a touch more water and blend again to combine. Add more salt, olive oil, garlic or lemon to taste.

Baba ganoush

2 large aubergines

1 clove of garlic, crushed

Juice of half a lemon

2 tsp tahini

½ tsp ground cumin

½ tsp ground coriander

Splash of extra virgin olive oil

Salt and pepper, to taste

Prick the aubergine with a fork and place under a hot grill, or bake in the oven at 180°C until the skins go black and the flesh is soft, or for up to half an hour.

Scoop out the flesh, discarding the skins, and place all of the ingredients in a blender and blitz until smooth. Taste and adjust seasoning if necessary.

Drizzle with a little more olive oil if desired.

Tzatziki

½ cucumber, peeled, deseeded and grated

½ tsp salt

150g Greek yoghurt

1 clove of garlic, crushed

1 tsp lemon juice

1 tbsp mint, chopped

Put grated cucumber in a sieve with the salt, and place over a bowl. Put a plate on top of the sieve and let the water drain out of the cucumber for at least half an hour. Pat the cucumber dry.

Put all the ingredients apart from the oil in a bowl, mix and season to taste. Drizzle with olive oil before serving if desired.

Difficulty: ● ● ○ ○ ○
Preparation time: 10 mins
Cooking time: 30 mins

Serving: 4

Storage: Store in an airtight container in the fridge for up to three days. Tzatziki best eaten fresh.

Recipe by **Mel Taylor**

Mel is a cook and runs a locally
based, mobile food business
called Gopal's Curry Shack.

UNDER 30 MINS

Leek & onion bhajis with yoghurt dip

I love making bhajis because they are so versatile. You can make them with most vegetables and it is a really tasty way to use up veg from your garden or veg box.

Ingredients

1 medium leek, halved lengthways, washed and finely sliced

1 small onion, peeled and finely sliced

2 cloves of garlic, finely chopped

1 green chilli, finely chopped

150g gram flour (chickpea flour)

½ tsp salt

2 tbsp coriander, chopped

1 tsp turmeric

½ tsp black onion seeds

1 tsp garam masala

1 tsp ground cumin

1 tsp ground coriander

¼ tsp bicarbonate of soda

100ml water

Sunflower oil for frying

For the yoghurt & coriander dip

45g pot of plain natural yoghurt

1 spring onion, finely sliced

2 tsp coriander, chopped

1 sprig of mint, finely chopped

¼ clove of garlic, finely chopped/grated

Method

To make the yoghurt dip, mix all the ingredients together in a bowl and set aside.

Place all the bhaji ingredients, excluding water and oil, into a large bowl and mix together well. Add enough water to make the mixture come together and combine by adding a little at a time. The mixture should stick together so that you can form balls or clumps with your hands. If you add too much water, just add a little more gram flour to thicken the mixture again.

Pour the sunflower oil in a large pan or deep fat fryer, to about a 5cm depth. Heat the oil until it is hot enough to brown a cube of bread.

Very carefully drop large tablespoons of the mixture into the oil. Fry each bhaji for 3 to 4 minutes until golden brown, turning with a slotted metal spoon halfway through cooking.

Remove from the pan with the slotted spoon and drain on kitchen paper.

Serve immediately with the yoghurt dip, lemon wedges and a crisp green salad.

TOP TIP

Once cooled, line a funnel with kitchen paper, place over a clean bottle and pour in the frying oil. This will filter it for re-use.

Difficulty: ●●○○○
Preparation time: 15 mins
Cooking time: 5 mins

Serving: Makes 8-12 bhajis

Storage: Best eaten fresh.

THE
**FISH
SHOP**

All our fish and seafood is
Guaranteed fresh. Ethically sourced.
and delivered daily from the fish markets
Corr... Devon. ...receiving

ZAMBURIÑAS
en salsa de vieira
diamir.
£2.99
ZAMBURIÑAS

Díam
Cojo

*entos
del Piquillo*
ENTEROS 8/12
PRODUCTO ARTESANO
Especial para rellenos

The Fish Shop

143 Gloucester Road BS7 8BA
www.lovethefishshop.com

Started on a whim in 2009, **The Fish Shop** is the brainchild of Dan Stern who surprisingly knew little about his craft when he started the business. However, with lots of fish-eating experience and three years under his belt now, his leap of faith worked out well and business is booming on Gloucester Road where Dan loves the sheer diversity of the shops and businesses.

As specialists in south coast dayboat fish and with a selection of shellfish, seafood and smoked fish on display daily, customers come from as far as Chippenham and Gloucester to buy the freshest fish around from Dan and his team of merry fishmongers.

With a huge focus on sustainability, Dan is often able to tell customers where and how his produce was caught and can even offer recipes and advice on prep and cooking with fish. "It's simple," says Dan. "We sell what we like to eat."

Ceviche

An easy to make dish which makes an impressive starter any time of the year and relies heavily on "cooking" really fresh fish in lime juice. You can make ceviche with any fish. Here The Fish Shop have used sea bass, but bream, mackerel or herrings make a good alternative.

Ingredients

2 fillets of sea bass
(around 250g in total),
skinned and pin-boned

Juice of two limes

1 clove of garlic,
finely chopped

20 cherry tomatoes,
quartered

Half a small red onion,
roughly chopped

1 red·chilli, roughly
chopped

Good handful
of coriander,
roughly chopped

For the tortillas

100g plain flour

50g polenta

100ml cold water

1 tbsp olive oil

Pinch of salt

Method

Chop the fish into 2cm squares and mix thoroughly with the garlic and lime juice in a small bowl. Leave to marinate while you make the tortillas. Marinate for up to an hour – the longer the fish is left in contact with the acid in the lime juice, the more 'cooked' and firmer it will be. If you want a softer texture, marinate for no longer than 10 minutes and serve straight away.

To prepare the tortilla dough, mix all the tortilla ingredients together in a mixing bowl and knead for a few minutes on a lightly floured surface. You will be left with a slightly gritty paste. Take a small piece about half the size of a golf ball and roll it out on a floured surface until flat and 3-4mm thick. This should give you a tortilla of about 8cm in diameter.

Heat a non-stick frying pan with a small amount of oil and fry the tortillas for about 3-4 minutes each side until they bubble and go brown. Keep in a warm oven until they are ready to eat.

Combine the tomatoes, onion, chilli and coriander with the marinated fish and transfer to a serving dish. Remove the tortillas from the oven and eat together.

Difficulty: ● ● ○ ○ ○
Preparation time: 20 minutes
(tortillas), min 10 minutes (ceviche)
Cooking time: 10 minutes

Serving: 4 for a starter or 2 for a main course.

Storage: Best eaten fresh.

Recipe by **Lizzie Davis**

Lizzie is an arts journalist who can usually be found in one of Bristol's theatres or concert halls.

UNDER 30 MINS

Salade de chèvre chaud

V

I adore France – for its wine, its summers, its language, its art. And, of course, for its cheese. This is an incredibly simple recipe which I make when I want to metaphorically whisk myself across the Channel for the evening. For me, this is France on a plate...

Ingredients

2 little gem lettuces, washed

10 cherry tomatoes, halved

50g pine nuts (or walnuts)

200g goats cheese with rind

French baguette, sliced

For the dressing

3 tbsp extra virgin olive oil

1 tbsp balsamic vinegar

1 tsp basil, chopped

Method

Put the lettuce and cherry tomatoes in a large bowl.

Heat the pine nuts in a dry frying pan for about a minute, or until slightly browned.

Prepare the dressing by mixing together the olive oil, balsamic vinegar and basil.

Add the pine nuts to the bowl with the lettuce and tomatoes. Pour the dressing over all the ingredients and toss.

Slice the goats cheese into pieces about 1cm thick and cut the bread into small slices. Put a piece of goats cheese on each piece of bread and place under a warm grill for around 5 minutes.

Serve the salad onto two plates, placing the bread and goats cheese on top.

Ét voila!

Difficulty: ●○○○○
Preparation time: 10 mins
Cooking time: 5 mins

Serving: 2

Storage: Best eaten fresh.

The main event

Recipe by **Kate Debley**

Kate recently added a baby to her
menagerie in Ashley Down.

Tuscan-style chicken

My mum came up with this recipe for a fundraising
'Tuscan' evening a few years ago, and it is now
a firm favourite with family and friends.

Ingredients

4 large potatoes, peeled
and cut into 2cm cubes

12 skinless, boneless
chicken thighs

3 tbsp olive oil

1 large red onion,
coarsely chopped

6 sprigs of rosemary,
pulled into smaller pieces

1 unwaxed lemon, finely
chopped (including skin)

2 tbsp balsamic vinegar

500g cherry tomatoes

Salt and pepper

Method

Preheat oven to 200°C.

Bring a pan of salted water to the boil.
Add the cubed potatoes, cook until fluffy
and drain.

Cut the chicken thighs into four or five pieces
each and coat the pieces with 1 tablespoon of
the olive oil. Mix with the onion and place in
an ovenproof dish (approximately 25x35x4cm
deep). Season well. Add the rosemary and
scatter the cooked potato followed by the
lemon pieces. Drizzle with the balsamic
vinegar and the remaining olive oil.

Put in the oven and cook for 30 minutes
before adding the tomatoes to the dish.
Do not stir them in. Return to the oven for a
further 20-30 minutes until the potatoes are
golden and the lemon pieces caramelised.

Remove from the oven and allow to cool
a little before serving. The dish tastes best
when served warm but not piping hot.

Serve with a green salad.

Difficulty: ●●○○○
Preparation time: 20 mins
Cooking time: 1 hour

Serving: 4-6

Storage: Keep in fridge for up to
three days. Reheat thoroughly.

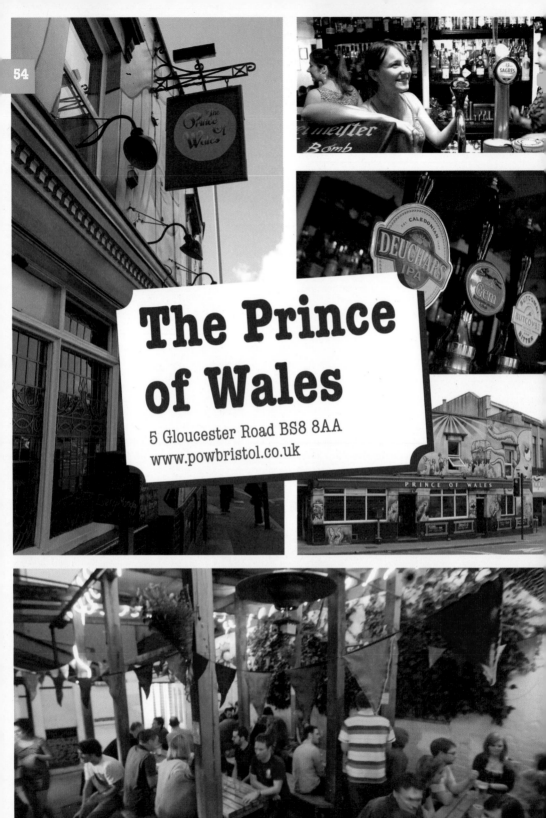

The Prince of Wales

5 Gloucester Road BS8 8AA
www.powbristol.co.uk

DRINK MORE GIN

From the grafitti on the front and the handmade bunting lining the garden, you'd be forgiven for thinking of **The Prince Of Wales** as just another student pub, but appearances can definitely be deceptive. Frequented by mid-twenties to thirty-somethings enjoying a post-work pint, the odd lone gentleman reading his newspaper and families at the weekends, The Prince Of Wales is full of the friendliness, character and charm that Gloucester Road has become famous for. "Gloucester Road is all about knowing the faces and the regulars," says Imogen, the pub's longest-standing manager. "Although we're technically rivals, all of the bars are different and keen to help each other out. It's lovely!"

With a close-knit family of staff who have great fun working under her wing, Anna Madams is The Prince Of Wales' owner of ten years who is keen to supply her customers with a steady stream of local ales and ciders (the most local of which come from just up the road at Ashley Down Brewery) and an impressive and completely under-rated food menu with ingredients sourced locally where possible. So whether you like bar snacks with your pint or a three course meal with wine, pop down to POW.

Caribbean brown chicken stew, rice & peas

Make the time to marinate this dish from The Prince of Wales and this will be a fantastic, sticky, spicy chicken stew with a bit of a kick.

OVERNIGHTER

Ingredients

8 chicken thighs

For the seasoning

1 tsp curry powder

1 tsp jerk seasoning

1 tsp thyme

1 tsp dry chicken stock

1 tsp mixed spice

1 tsp paprika

1 pinch grated nutmeg

Juice of a lemon

2 tsp soy sauce

3 cloves of garlic, finely chopped

2cm of root ginger, peeled and grated

1 large onion, chopped

1 red pepper, deseeded and diced

For the stew

Sunflower oil

2 tsp sugar

3 tomatoes, diced

2 tsp tomato purée

1 litre of water

40g piece of creamed coconut block

1 tsp chicken stock

1 scotch bonnet chilli

For the rice and peas

1 onion, peeled and finely chopped

2 cloves of garlic, peeled and finely chopped

300g long grain rice

400ml tin coconut milk

600ml vegetable stock

1 tsp thyme, leaves only, chopped

400g tin red kidney beans

1 tbsp olive oil

Method

Add the seasoning ingredients to a large bowl and stir well. Add the chicken, coating each piece well and leave to marinate overnight in the fridge.

Heat the sunflower oil with the sugar over a medium heat until the sugar is brown. Add the chicken, leaving the seasoning ingredients in the bowl at this point. Allow the chicken to brown for 3-4 minutes on each side before adding the seasoning from the bowl and cooking for a further 3 minutes.

Stir in the tomatoes and tomato purée and cook for a further 3-5 minutes until the tomatoes are soft. Add the water, creamed coconut, stock and the chilli.

Bring to the boil then reduce the heat and simmer for an hour, stirring occasionally and skimming any excess oil which may rise to the top of stew.

For the rice and peas: Heat the oil in a large saucepan and fry the onion over a medium heat for around 5 minutes, until softened and beginning to brown, stirring occasionally. Add the garlic and stir in the rice, ensuring it is coated well with the oil. Pour in the coconut milk and vegetable stock and add the thyme leaves.

Bring to the boil then reduce the heat and place a lid on the pan. Cook gently for 15 minutes until the rice is cooked through and the liquid is all absorbed.

Stir in the kidney beans and warm through for a further five minutes.

Serve the rice and peas with the chicken stew.

Difficulty: ● ● ● ○ ○
Preparation time: Overnight
Cooking time: 1 hour

Serving: 4

Storage: Will keep in fridge for three days. Chicken stew suitable for freezing, use within a month and reheat thoroughly.

Recipe by **Jane Bowyer**

Jane lives in St Andrews and enjoys
having the unique Gloucester Road
on her doorstep.

Oven-fried chicken

This versatile family favourite makes a great supper dish and is equally good cold for a picnic or packed lunch.

D

Ingredients

2 tbsp plain flour

Salt and pepper

6 chicken thighs and/or drumsticks

1 tbsp olive oil

100ml chicken stock

For the spicy seasoning

½ tsp English mustard powder

½ tsp chilli powder

½ tsp cayenne pepper

For the lemon and thyme seasoning

1 tsp thyme

1 tsp lemon zest

Method

Preheat oven to 180°C.

To prepare the seasoned flour mix, add the flour, salt and pepper and your choice of seasoning to a bowl. Stir well.

Trim the chicken of any extra fat, then one at a time, coat in the flour mix. Put the coated chicken pieces into a roasting tray greased with the oil and cook in the oven for around 30 minutes, until the juices run clear when the meat is pierced with the tip of a sharp knife. Baste the meat with the juices in the tray during cooking.

Once cooked, transfer the chicken pieces to a warmed dish and keep warm.

To make a gravy, mix any remaining flour mix with hot chicken stock to form a thin batter. Add this to the roasting tray and cook over a low heat, stirring constantly until the gravy reaches a simmering point. Allow to simmer for 2-3 minutes until thickened.

Serve the chicken with the gravy, potatoes and green vegetables, or without the gravy with salad.

Difficulty: ●●○○○
Preparation time: 10 mins
Cooking time: 30 mins

Serving: 2-4

Storage: Eat hot or cold within two days. Chicken can be frozen for up to a month if defrosted and reheated throroughly.

Recipe by **Leah Lewington**

Leah is an accountant who lives with her husband and loves to cook for her friends and family.

Turkey meatballs with spaghetti

Ⓓ

This is one of my favourite childhood dishes from when I was growing up. I used to help my mum make them and and we loved eating this dish at family meal times. Turkey is a great alternative for those who don't eat red meat.

For the tomato sauce

1 tbsp olive oil
1 small onion, peeled and chopped
2-3 cloves of garlic, peeled and chopped
½ fresh chilli, chopped
2 x 400g tins chopped tomatoes
1 tbsp smoked paprika
1 tsp sugar
Small bunch of fresh basil
Salt and pepper

For the meatballs

1 small onion, chopped
½ fresh chilli, chopped
A handful of fresh thyme, chopped
500g turkey mince (use beef, lamb or pork if preferred)
1 tsp smoked paprika
Salt and pepper
2 tbsp olive oil
Parmesan

Method

To make the tomato sauce: Heat the oil in a pan then add the onion and garlic, gently frying over a medium heat for 2-3 minutes until soft. Stir in the chilli. Add the chopped tomatoes, paprika and sugar and bring to the boil. Reduce to a low heat and simmer uncovered for 20 minutes, stirring occasionally. Add salt and pepper to taste.

To make the meatballs: Tip the onion, chilli and thyme into a bowl and add the turkey mince, paprika and a good pinch of salt and pepper. Mix all the ingredients together well until evenly distributed.

Take approximately a tablespoon of the mixture at a time and roll into meatballs until all of the mixture is used up.

Heat the oil in a large non-stick frying pan, add the meatballs and fry in batches over a medium heat for 10-15 minutes, turning occasionally to ensure all sides are golden brown and evenly cooked.

Once cooked, the meatballs can be added to the tomato sauce. Warm through in the tomato sauce for a further 5 minutes over a low heat.

Stir through the freshly chopped basil and serve with linguine or spaghetti and freshly grated Parmesan.

Difficulty: ●●○○○
Preparation time: 25 mins
Cooking time: 30 mins

Serving: 4

Storage: The meatballs and sauce can be frozen once cooked or store cooked in fridge for three days.

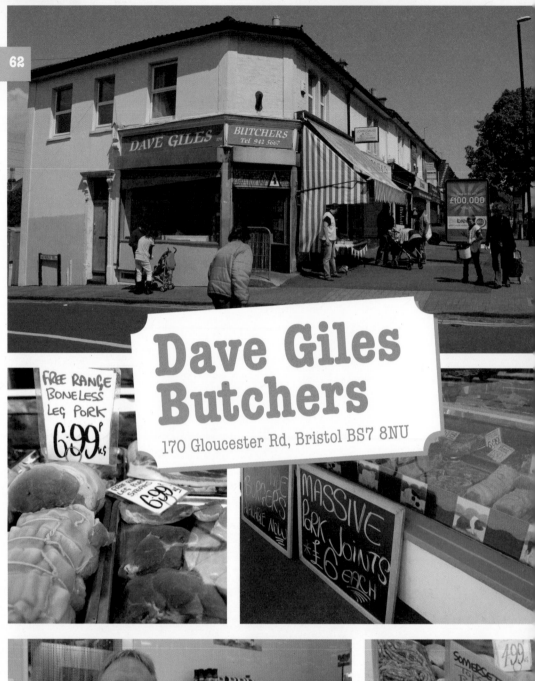

Dave Giles Butchers

170 Gloucester Rd, Bristol BS7 8NU

As one of those shops that carnivores can never walk past without popping in, **Dave Giles Butchers** is a family run business at its best. Selling all of the ordinary produce sold in a butcher's shop, Dave also sells cheese, eggs, milk and a great range of preserves and chutneys. With seasonal homemade sausages and burgers that keep the customers flocking, Dave's legendary pork joints for just £6 are also well known in the area for providing local residents with perfect Sunday lunches!

With most of his produce free range and coming from local farms, Dave also sells organic meat. He is just one of a handful of butchers left in Bristol who still buys in bodies of beef and cuts it up himself rather than buying pre-cut boxes. His customers love the honest, local produce he sells and they are his favourite thing about working on Gloucester Road. "It sounds a bit corny but the people round here are such nice people. Everyone's friendly and it's just a lovely place to be."

Classic Sunday roast with all the trimmings

Being a Yorkshire lass, the pudding recipe was a closely guarded family secret but, after agreeing with my mum, I've chosen to share the recipe with you. I believe the success of a roast is all in the timing and then the gravy; the rest is down to personal preference.

Ingredients

2-3kg rib of beef
Salt and pepper
Vegetable oil
3 small onions, peeled
Small handful of cherry tomatoes
A whole bulb of garlic
1kg of potatoes, washed and chopped
3 tbsp goose fat
50g Parmesan, finely grated
250ml beef stock
150ml red wine

For 24 small Yorkshire puddings

3 large eggs
200g plain flour
300ml milk
Pinch of salt
Lard/beef dripping

Note: Animal fats can be swapped with vegetable or sunflower oil.

Method

Bring the beef to room temperature before starting. Rub with salt, pepper and the vegetable oil and allow to rest.

Preheat oven to 170ºC.

For the beef: On the hob, seal the beef by frying it fat side down in a very hot pan, turning regularly until slightly browned on all sides. This should take around 5 minutes. Place the joint in a large roasting tray, fat side up and add the onions, tomatoes and garlic cloves (leave them in their skins). Cover the tray with foil and place it in the oven.

Cooking times vary depending on size of the joint but the general rule is 15 minutes per 450g for rare, 20 for medium and 25-30 for well done.

For the Yorkshire puddings: To prepare the batter, beat the eggs into the flour using a food processor or whisk, then gradually add the milk until the batter is lump-free. Season with salt. Set aside until you're ready to bake.

For the potatoes: Put the potatoes, skin on, in a roasting tray with the goose fat. Season and place in the oven with the meat. Roast the potatoes for at least an hour, turning occasionally. After half an hour, give the potatoes a shuffle to make sure all sides are cooking in the fat, sprinkle generously with Parmesan and return to the oven.

WINE MATCH A lovely, full bodied cabernet shiraz such as Passion Has Red Lips from Some Young Punks, South Australia, is a rather special bottle that we've chosen to go with this rich dinner. See p172 for more wine matching ideas.

Beef and potatoes: Once the beef is done, remove from the oven and leave to rest for at least 20 minutes before serving. Remove the potatoes at the same time and cover them with foil to keep warm.

Yorkshire puddings: Increase the heat on the oven to its maximum, 230°C if possible. Place a little lard in each of the holes in two muffin trays and put on the top two shelves of the oven. When the fat is almost smoking, pour the batter into the holes, quickly returning the trays to the top of the oven for 20 minutes.

Gravy: Whilst the meat is resting and the Yorkshires are in, prepare the gravy. Using the tray the beef was cooked in, remove all but one of the roasted onions to serve separately, leaving the tomatoes and garlic. Pour in the beef stock and cook over a low heat. Stir using a potato masher, mashing the tomatoes and garlic and absorbing all the cooked meat juices from the pan. Add the wine and return to a simmer. When your preferred consistency has been achieved (add a teaspoon of flour to thicken it up if needed), give everything another mash and pour the gravy through a sieve into a jug to remove the garlic skins and tomato seeds.

Yorkshire puddings: When ready, the Yorkshire puddings should be puffed up, big and golden dark brown. They can be reheated in the oven if needed for a couple of minutes before serving, or made in advance.

To serve: Carve the beef. Serve with vegetables of your choice (it goes really well with the red cabbage recipe on p124). Present your beautiful Yorkshire puddings and crisp roasties then smother everything with gravy and enjoy!

TOP TIP

You could have the Yorkshire puddings the traditional way, as a starter with a bit of gravy. This was done to fill people up in days of old so they wouldn't eat so much of the expensive meat.

Difficulty: ● ● ● ○ ○
Preparation time: 20 mins
Cooking time: 2 hours

Serving: 6-8 people.

Storage: Keep leftovers in fridge up to two days, reheat in microwave or oven thoroughly. Yorkshire pudding can be stored for up to a month in the freezer.

Recipe by **India Rabey**

India is a freelance graphic
designer who lives in Horfield
with her husband and giant dog.

Rib of beef by
DAVE GILES

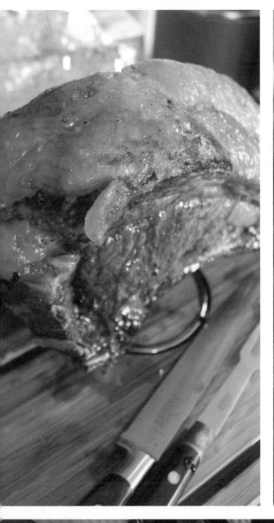

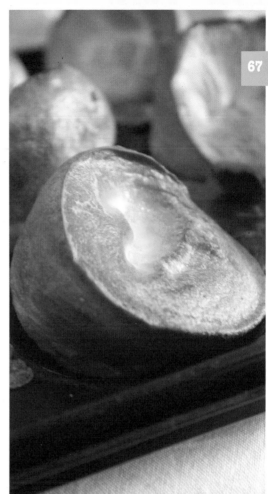

Recipe by **Nikki Morgans**

Busy Nikki works full time, runs a
charity and is also completing a BSc.
She lives in Westbury-On-Trym.

Beef jambalaya

My friend Sasha has cooked this for us a few times and it's lovely. It's proper comfort food and a real good feed. It's really easy to make, done in one pan and is a sociable dish; enjoy with good friends and good wine.

Ingredients

550g sirloin or fillet steak

200g cooking chorizo, sliced

5 tbsp olive oil

2 peppers, deseeded and diced

3 celery sticks, chopped

1 large onion, sliced

6 cloves of garlic, chopped

600g long grain rice, rinsed

2 tbsp tomato puree

1 red chilli, chopped

2 tbsp ground ginger

1 tbsp Cajun seasoning

400g tin of chopped tomatoes

1 litre chicken stock

24 large raw tiger prawns

Salt and pepper

Method

Season the steaks with salt and pepper. Leave to rest.

Using the biggest pan you have, or a paella pan, fry the chorizo in one or two tablespoons of the oil over a medium heat until golden.

Stir in the peppers and celery. Cook to soften for 5-10 minutes, being careful to watch the heat in case they begin to catch and burn. Reduce the heat slightly if necessary. Remove the chorizo, peppers and celery from the pan and set aside.

Add more oil to the pan if necessary and fry the onion for 5 minutes until softened. Then add the garlic, rice, tomato purée, chilli, ginger and Cajun spice and stir for 2 minutes until the rice is translucent and covered in the spices. Stir in the chopped tomatoes and the stock. Season with salt and bring to the boil. Turn the heat right down, put the pan lid on (if you have one) and allow to simmer for around 20 minutes until the rice is tender, stirring occasionally to avoid sticking. Add a little boiling water if the mixture begins to dry out.

Meanwhile, fry the steaks to your liking: 2 minutes either side for rare and 5 minutes either side for medium.

When the rice is cooked, stir in the prawns and heat through for a few minutes until the prawns have all turned pink. Check the seasoning, add the chorizo, celery and pepper mixture and stir well. Slice the steak and add it to the rice, stirring thoroughly until piping hot throughout.

Serve with wedges of lime, salad and sour cream, putting the big pan right in the middle of the table so that everyone can help themselves.

Difficulty: ● ● ● ○ ○
Preparation time: 15 mins
Cooking time: 45 mins

Serving: 8

Storage: Best eaten fresh.

SLOW COOKED

Recipe by
Danielle Coombs

Danielle is a freelance chef and
runs Bishopston Supper Club.

Wild rabbit braised in cider

Tasty rabbit is abundant, good value and enjoying a resurgence in popularity. This slow-cooked autumnal recipe really brings the flavour out of the meat.

Ingredients

1 thick slice of pancetta or 4 rashers streaky bacon, cut into chunks

1 medium sized rabbit, skinned, gutted and jointed (ask the butcher)

50g plain flour, seasoned with salt and pepper

1 medium onion

1 carrot

1 leek

2 sticks of celery

2 cloves of garlic

1 sprig of thyme

1 sprig of rosemary

1 bay leaf

5 peppercorns

1 pint dry cider

50ml double cream

1 dessertspoon wholegrain mustard (optional)

A handful of dried ceps (optional)

Method

Brown the pancetta/bacon pieces in a dry frying pan over a medium heat then remove from the pan and set aside.

Coat the rabbit pieces in the seasoned flour and brown in the same pan over a medium heat, using the fat left over from the pancetta/bacon, before transferring to a large saucepan or casserole dish.

Roughly chop the vegetables and add to the dish along with the garlic, herbs, peppercorns and cider. Add just enough cold water to cover the rabbit and vegetables. Bring to almost boiling, skim off any froth from the surface and reduce the heat to a slow simmer. Cover and cook for approximately 2 hours, either over a low heat on the hob or in a preheated oven at 120ºC, until the meat is tender and falling off the bone.

Strain the liquid from the casserole and set aside. Remove the meat from the bones and also set aside. Discard the vegetables and herbs.

Return the liquid to the pan and over a low/medium heat, reduce the stock by at least half. This will take at least 30 minutes. Then stir in the cream, mustard, cooked pancetta and ceps and continue to reduce until the sauce is thickened and glossy.

Return the meat to the sauce and warm through. Season to taste.

Serve with creamy, mashed or new potatoes, and greens.

Difficulty: ● ● ● ○ ○
Preparation time: 15 mins
Cooking time: 2-3 hours

Serving: 4

Storage: Keep covered in fridge for three days. Suitable for freezing, use within a month and reheat thoroughly.

Atomic Burger

189 Gloucester Road BS7 8BG
www.atomicburger.co.uk

Atomic Burger is, put quite simply, a lot of fun. With emphasis placed just as much on the experience as on the food, owner Martin Bunce and his team take you back to your childhood with hundreds of nostalgic references from the worlds of TV, film, comic books and video games covering the diner-style restaurant. "It's an Aladdin's cave of memories and really cool junk," says Martin.

"We just want people to have a great time – just sit back and relax and have a fantastic burger."

The food itself extends the theme with the whole menu being named after iconic actors and characters. Their American-style burgers piled high with toppings ensure you will never leave Atomic Burger hungry, especially if you try one of their famous milkshakes or their delicious roasty toasty marshmallows for pud.

After opening in early 2012 as their first foray outside of Oxford, Atomic Burger were welcomed with open arms into Bristol's foodie scene and Martin, like many others, loves the independent spirit in the area. "We wouldn't fit in in a faceless shopping street. We are passionate about what we do and I believe Gloucester Road demands that."

SLOW COOKED

Perfect BBQ pulled pork

Pulled pork is a wonderful, versatile meat that can be served hot or cold, as part of a sandwich or wrap. This recipe from Atomic Burger allows you to make perfect pulled pork using your oven; you don't need a smoker, barbecue or any technical equipment – just a lot of love and patience for this slow-roasted southern delight.

Barbecue sauce

250ml tomato ketchup
2 large cloves of garlic, crushed
2 tbsp dark brown sugar
1 tbsp maple syrup
2 tbsp Worcestershire sauce
2 tbsp cider vinegar
1 tsp smoked paprika
Ground black pepper

For the dry rub

3 tbsp smoked paprika
1 tbsp garlic salt
1 tbsp light brown sugar
3 tbsp sea salt
4 tbsp plain flour

Pulled pork

2.5kg-4kg boned pork shoulder joint, trimmed of surface fat
150ml amber beer or pale ale

Method

The barbecue sauce can be prepared in advance. Place ingredients into a small pan and cook over a medium heat for around 20 minutes until the sauce thickens, stirring frequently. Remove from the heat and allow to cool.

Preheat oven to 150°C.

Combine the dry rub ingredients in a small bowl and mix well. Massage into the outside of the joint, working the flavours into the meat. Ideally, cover and refrigerate the joint for 24 hours to create a deeper flavour, although this is not essential.

Place the joint into a large roasting tin and pour the amber beer around the joint, taking care not to pour it over the top.

Completely cover the roasting tin in foil to create a seal, allowing the juices and flavours to cook into the meat. Roast the joint for 2 hours.

Remove the foil and return to the oven for a further two hours, allowing the remaining liquid to partly evaporate and create a crisp crust on the joint.

Remove from the oven and transfer to a plate. Allow the joint to rest uncovered for 10 minutes. Whilst the meat is still warm, take two forks and strip the meat into shreds, using one fork to hold the meat in place and the other to separate the meat. Place the shredded meat into a bowl and mix with the barbecue sauce and any meat juices from the joint.

Serve in a lightly toasted bun with coleslaw and pickles.

Difficulty: ●●●○○
Preparation time: 20 mins
Cooking time: 4 hours

Serving: 12

Storage: Will last three days in fridge. Use leftover barbecue sauce as a burger topping or marinade for summer barbecue meats.

Recipe by **Amanda Clarke**

Amanda is an accountant and lives
in Bishopston with her husband.

Chorizo, mushroom and pea risotto

This is a warming and filling recipe that is lovely to make on a day when you've got a bit of time to spend in the kitchen, stirring away and dancing around to the radio!

Ingredients

150g chorizo, chopped

150g mushrooms, chopped

2 tbsp olive oil

1 large onion, peeled and chopped

2 cloves of garlic, peeled and finely chopped

300g risotto rice

125ml white wine

1 litre chicken or vegetable stock

2 handfuls of frozen peas, about 100g

20g butter

100g Parmesan, grated

Juice of a lemon

Small handful of parsley and/or basil, roughly chopped

Salt and pepper

Method

Fry the chorizo in a dry pan over a medium heat until it is starting to brown and crisp up around the edges. Set aside. In the same pan, fry the mushrooms until they soften and take on some of the colour and flavour of the chorizo. Set aside with the chorizo.

Heat the olive oil in a large wide-based pan and add the onions. Sweat over a low heat for around five minutes until the onions are softened. Add the garlic and cook for a further minute.

Add the risotto rice to the pan and stir in well for a couple of minutes. Pour in the wine and stir until it has evaporated. Add the stock a ladleful at a time, stirring regularly until each ladleful has been absorbed by the rice. Continue until the rice is cooked but al dente – this should take around 20 minutes.

Add the frozen peas along with the butter and the Parmesan and stir well. Stir in the chorizo and mushrooms then add the lemon juice. If the risotto is too thick, add a little extra water or stock to loosen it. Season to taste. Stir in the chopped herbs and serve straight away with a green salad.

TOP TIP

Use warm stock as the rice will absorb this quicker and more easily.

Difficulty: ●●○○○
Preparation time: 10 mins
Cooking time: 30 mins

Serving: 4

Storage: Best eaten fresh.

The Gallimaufry

26 The Promenade, Gloucester Road BS7 8AE
www.thegallimaufry.co.uk

To the prominent space that was vacated by The Prom five days earlier came a new group of faces in March 2012 when **The Gallimaufry** opened their doors to the masses.

Run by James Koch and head chef John Watson, the 'home-cooking and curios bar' brings the feel of a pub with a difference to Gloucester Road. The Gallimaufry serves up delightful home-cooking inspired dishes from a doorstep sandwich for lunch to seasonal stews or salads for dinner, and an extensive drinks menu featuring a great wine selection, real ales, ciders and plenty of unusual spirits. "Our staff have a knowledge of, and interest in our menu and will happily knock you up a killer cocktail!" says James.

In quirky surroundings with a colourful Dave Bain mural along the back of the wall, the Galli is a place for all things fun and nearly everything on display is for sale from the handmade lamps and dolls to the furniture. They are dedicated to promoting emerging artists and craftspeople and have nightly live music offerings from open mic to bands and DJs. The bar is also a Bristol Pound Access Point where you can exchange Sterling into Bristol Pounds to spend in participating businesses around the city.

Braised pork belly and cuttlefish broth

Ingredients

2kg piece of pork belly

5 star anise

10 peppercorns

1 medium cuttlefish or squid (main body 6-8 inches), cleaned and prepared

3 tsp olive oil

4 banana shallots, or a small onion, finely diced

250ml fish stock

250ml chicken stock

50ml Pernod

100ml white wine

150g Chantenay carrots, quartered

150g baby turnips, quartered

Handful of radishes, quartered

1 small handful of flat leaf parsley

1 Granny Smith apple, peeled and cut into small cubes

TOP TIP

Ask your fishmonger to clean and prepare your cuttlefish to save time and mess!

Difficulty: ● ● ● ● ○

Preparation time: 8 hours braising plus 2 hours pressing

Cooking time: 10 mins pork, 2hrs cuttlefish

Serving: 4

Storage: Keep in fridge and eat within three days. Reheat thoroughly. Pork only can be frozen.

Method

Pork belly: Put the belly in a roasting tray, cover with water, add the star anise and peppercorns, tightly seal the tray with foil and cook in the oven for 8 hours on the lowest heat, about 90-100°C. (This can be done overnight.)

Remove the tray from the oven and allow to cool to just above room temperature, still covered. Remove the belly, strain and discard the spices and reserve the stock. Skim any excess fat off the top of the pork stock and chill until required.

When cool enough to handle, twist any bones out of the belly making sure that all the bone has been removed each time. Remove any excess fat from the bottom of the belly. Place the joint on a tray in between two sheets of greaseproof paper, place another tray on top and transfer to the fridge and put a heavy weight on top – for example, a couple of tins of tomatoes. Chill for 2-3 hours until firm and compacted. Remove from fridge, trim, and slice into neat portions.

Cuttlefish stew: Open the main body of the cuttlefish out like a book on a chopping board with the outer surface facing up. Cut the tentacles in half and remove the beak and any larger, chewier suckers (on the end of the two long tentacles). With a sharp knife score the whole meat diagonally, cutting just into the flesh and not entirely through it. Cut into approximately 3cm strips. Season with salt and pepper.

Heat a heavy-based saucepan, add a teaspoon of oil and sauté the shallot/onion over a medium heat until soft. Add the fish stock, chicken stock and 200ml of the pork stock reserved from earlier. Bring to a simmer and add the cuttlefish tentacles.

Heat the other teaspoon of oil in a large frying pan and fry the rest of the seasoned cuttlefish until golden. Add the Pernod, which deglazes the pan to lift off any cuttlefish juices stuck to the bottom. Add the white wine when the Pernod starts to thicken and add the entire contents of the pan to the broth. Cook over a low heat with a lid on for 2 hours and check for seasoning.

Before serving: Preheat oven to 190°C. Season both sides of the pork belly. Heat a frying pan over a medium heat, add a little oil and fry the pork belly, skin down, until golden brown and crispy. Turn over, place on a baking tray and finish cooking in the oven for 10 minutes.

Meanwhile, add the vegetables to the broth and cook for around 10 minutes on a simmer until the vegetables are tender but still with a bit of bite. Add a handful of roughly chopped parsley and the apple cubes at the end.

Serve in large bowls with the belly in the centre surrounded by the broth.

Recipe by Claire Groom

Claire is an opera singer and singing
teacher. She lives in St Andrews.

SLOW COOKED

Moroccan lamb tagine

This is my favourite recipe ever! Delicious, simple, flavour-packed comfort food. It will fill the whole house with the scent of cinnamon and orange.

Ingredients

2 tbsp olive oil

550g lean lamb, trimmed of fat and cubed

2 onions, chopped

3 garlic cloves, crushed

700ml lamb or chicken stock

Grated zest and juice of 1 large orange

1 cinnamon stick

1 tsp ground ginger

2 tsp paprika

½ tsp cayenne pepper

1 tbsp clear honey

100g ready to eat semi-dried apricots, chopped

50g dates, chopped

3 tbsp fresh mint, chopped

25g ground almonds

25g flaked almonds

Salt and pepper

Method

Preheat oven to 160°C.

Heat the oil in a tagine or flame-proof casserole dish with a lid. Add the lamb and fry evenly over a medium heat with a pinch of salt, sealing on all sides. Remove from the pan and set aside on a plate.

Turn down the heat and gently fry the onions and garlic for a few minutes until golden and softened. Return the lamb to the pan then pour in the stock, zest, juice, spices, honey and seasoning. Bring it all to the boil then cover and cook in the oven for 2 hours or until the lamb is tender. Check occasionally to make sure it doesn't dry out, adding water if so.

Half an hour before the end, add the apricots, dates and two tablespoons of the mint.

Remove from the oven and stir in the ground almonds to thicken the sauce.

Scatter the remaining mint and toasted almonds over the top and serve with couscous or paprika-coated sweet potato wedges.

Difficulty: ●●○○○
Preparation time: 15 mins
Cooking time: 2½ hours

Serving: 4

Storage: Will keep in fridge for three days. Suitable for freezing, use within a month and reheat thoroughly.

84

Recipe by
Claire-Louise Partridge

CLP is a full-time planning manager,
wife and mum who loves cake and
has a PhD in molecular genetics.

Moussaka

I remember watching my old Greek flatmate make this –
it was his mum's recipe. I've adapted it a little so that it
can be made as either a vegetarian or non-vegetarian dish.
For me, it tastes of sunshine! It's one of those dishes that
improves with age and is best eaten with a green salad.

Ingredients

750g lamb mince
(or 500g vegetarian mince)

2 onions, finely chopped

1 carrot, diced

1 medium sweet
potato, diced

2 sticks celery, finely
chopped

4 cloves of garlic, crushed

¼ nutmeg, grated

1 tsp cinnamon

2 tsp fresh chopped
oregano or thyme

400g tin chopped plum
tomatoes

2 tbsp tomato purée

400ml lamb or
vegetable stock

500g courgette

500g potatoes

500g aubergine

Olive oil

Salt and pepper

3 eggs

400ml crème fraiche

250ml greek yoghurt

Feta cheese

Method

Preheat oven to 180°C.

In a large pan, dry fry the lamb mince until browned and
slightly crisp. Remove from pan and drain off any excess fat.

Add the onion, carrot, sweet potato and celery to the
same pan. Add a little olive oil and cook over a medium
heat for around 5 minutes until the vegetables are
starting to soften. Return the lamb mince to the pan, add
the garlic, spices and oregano and leave to cook for a few
minutes. Add the chopped tomatoes, tomato puree and
stock and leave to simmer for a further 15 minutes.
Set aside.

Meanwhile, slice the courgettes (5mm) potatoes (3mm)
and aubergine (1cm) lengthways. Paint them with a little
olive oil and either griddle, grill or bake them in batches
until golden and soft – a minute on each side on a
griddle (or in a dry frying pan), 5 minutes under the grill,
or up to 15 minutes in the oven.

Put a layer of the potatoes in the bottom of the
casserole dish and season with salt and pepper.
Cover with half of the mince mixture. Cover this with a
rough layer of aubergine, followed by courgette strips
and then potatoes, seasoning after each layer. Repeat
the mince layer then finish with a mixed layer of
courgettes and aubergine.

Beat the eggs together in a bowl and mix in the crème
fraiche and yoghurt. Season and pour over the layered
mixture. Spread evenly and then crumble feta cheese
over the top.

Bake for 40 minutes until golden brown on top.

Difficulty: ● ● ● ○ ○
Preparation time: 1 hour
Cooking time: 40 mins

Serving: 8

Storage: Will keep in fridge for
three days. Suitable for freezing
in portions, use within a month.
Reheat thoroughly.

Delmonico

217A Gloucester Road BS7 8NN
www.delmonico.co.uk

Marvellous Mocha Cake £1.95
or coffee + cake

A family-run business open for 12 years, **Delmonico** have recently had an overhaul and transformed their business from evening restaurant into a stunning all day eatery.

Serving a traditional brunch menu featuring dishes such as eggs florentine to lunchtime favourites including seasonal salads, sandwiches and the odd sharing platter, Delmonico's evening menu of European inspired British cuisine is no longer the only string to its bow. They even serve a daily selection of homemade cakes including their customers' old favourites – carrot cake and orange polenta cake. Visitors can dine alfresco in their outdoor eating area or even take advantage of 'The Library', Delmonico's private dining room on the restaurant's mezzanine floor.

Nick Hennessy, the owner and head chef lives in walking distance of the restaurant and loves the ever-present local vibe on Gloucester Road. "There's such a community feel here, we really look after our area. Being one of the traders on the road is great – there's definitely a sense of sticking together."

Haddock with a herb crust & pea purée

One of Delmonico's most popular dishes and a delicious modern twist on homemade fish 'n' chips.

Ingredients

200g peas

Olive oil

A few chopped mint leaves

Salt and pepper

100g day-old bread

2 large shallots or 1 onion, diced

Handful of chopped parsley

Dessertspoon of thyme

Dessertspoon of oregano

2 haddock portions

Method

Preheat oven to 220°C.

Bring a small pan of salted water to the boil and cook the peas for 5 minutes. Drain and return to the pan. Add a little olive oil and the mint, season and then roughly mash, and set aside.

Blend the bread in a food processor until you have fine crumbs (see page 176). Heat a little olive oil in a saucepan and cook the shallots until softened. Add the breadcrumbs and chopped herbs, season and mix to form a moist paste. Add more olive oil if necessary.

Season the fish with salt and pepper and place on a baking tray lined with baking paper. Spoon on the breadcrumb mix covering the fish and gently pat down with the back of the spoon. Bake for 8 minutes or until the crust is golden brown.

To serve, place pea purée neatly on a warm plate, using a round cutter to shape. Place the fish on top or just to the side of the peas and serve with hand cut chips or baked new potatoes.

Difficulty: ●●○○○
Preparation time: 10 mins
Cooking time: 8 minutes

Serving: 2

Storage: Best eaten fresh.

Recipe by **Ruth Wiles**

Ruth manages a wine shop in Westbury-on-Trym
and has loved Gloucester Road since the first
day she moved here four years ago.

Salmon en papillôte with tarragon butter

D

I love cooking this dinner for date-night as it's so tasty and simple that it's almost impossible to get wrong. Also, I'm a wine lover and this dish goes fantastically with one of my favourite wines – Chablis.

Ingredients

400g potatoes, peeled and halved

1 tbsp olive oil

Mixed herbs (marjoram, rosemary and sage work well), chopped

1 tsp fresh tarragon, chopped

Juice of a lemon

25g butter, softened

1 head of fennel, finely sliced

2 portions of salmon (approximately 160g each)

Salt and pepper

Method

Preheat oven to 190°C.

Parboil the potatoes in salted water until tender. Drain and add to a roasting tin. Drizzle with the oil and toss to coat the potatoes. Add the mixed herbs, season and place in the oven to roast.

To make the tarragon butter, mix the chopped tarragon and a little lemon juice into the butter and season.

Cut two squares (or discs) of foil or greaseproof paper. Place half of the sliced fennel in the middle of each and place each salmon portion on top of the fennel. Spoon half the tarragon butter on top of each piece of salmon, giving each a squeeze of lemon and seasoning with salt and pepper. Fold each piece of foil/paper into a neat parcel, folding the edges tightly to seal.

Place on a baking tray and bake for 8 minutes. Carefully open up the parcels; the salmon's flesh should be firm and pale when cooked, the fennel should be soft and the butter melted and coating everything.

Transfer to a warm plate and serve with the roasted herby potatoes.

Difficulty: ● ● ● ○ ○
Preparation time: 10 mins
Cooking time: 40 mins

Serving: 2

Storage: Best eaten fresh.

UNDER 30 MINS

Recipe by **Sara Budd**

Sara encourages her children in their
non-structured/autonomous home
education, which is NOT doing nothing!

Wasabi tuna fishcakes & guacamole

D

Hot fishcakes with cool guacamole.
Cook on the hob or great on the barbecue
if you like something a bit different.

Ingredients

1 level tsp wasabi paste
2 tsp Dijon mustard
½ tsp salt
1 tbsp chopped ginger
1½ tbsp sunflower oil
2-3 cloves of
garlic, chopped
450g fresh tuna, cut into
small steaks

For the guacamole:

An avocado, de-stoned
½ fresh red chilli
Juice of half a lemon
Handful of fresh coriander
½ red onion, chopped

Method

Combine all the fishcake ingredients in a food processor, pulsing until well mixed but chunky.

Form the mixture into 4-6 burger patties, depending on the size you'd like. Place on a plate and chill in the fridge for 20 minutes.

Heat a little oil in a frying pan before frying (you can also grill or barbecue them) for two minutes each side until golden brown and hot throughout.

Meanwhile, for the guacamole, blitz all the ingredients in a blender until almost smooth, adding a little water if the consistency is too thick.

Serve with lots of salad!

Difficulty: ●○○○○
Preparation time: 5 mins
Cooking time: 25 mins

Serving: 2-3 people, allowing two fishcakes for each person.

Storage: Best eaten fresh.

Pearce's

293 Gloucester Road BS7 8PE

As one of Gloucester Road's oldest and longest standing shops, **Pearce's** has been present as a family-run business for 120 years and was taken over 12 years ago by Michel and Paula Khan. The husband and wife team sell mops and buckets, toasters and kettles, mouse traps, draught excluders, glassware, kitchenware, plant food, chains and cords and absolutely everything in between. Proud of their one-stop status, Michel even insists that they will order in anything that they don't have.

The couple are committed to their work and spend so much time in their shop that they even have a full-size kitchen and garden there, prepped and ready for use! Comparing Gloucester Road to the traditional high street, Michel insists that the most important thing at Pearce's is the relationships with their customers. He says proudly, "I grew up in a market town where everybody knew each other and everybody helped each other out. If we didn't have something we'd send them somewhere else that did. We maintain that tradition at Pearce's today."

Vongolé á la Michel

Camp food isn't just for the holidays – cooking outdoors can be something special for wintery days as well as sizzling summer evenings. This recipe from Pearce's is perfect for cooking on a camping stove.

Ingredients

200g linguine

1 tbsp olive oil

3 shallots, finely diced

2 cloves of garlic, chopped

10-15 cherry tomatoes

50ml vermouth

Pinch of chilli powder

1kg of clams in shell (clean, debeard and discard any that aren't closed)

400g tin of shelled clams

200g crème fraiche (optional), or 50ml olive oil

Salt and pepper

Bunch of chopped flat leaf parsley, chopped

Method

Put the linguine in boiling water and cook for 10-12 minutes until al dénte.

Using a large pan with a lid, heat the oil and sauté the shallots and garlic over a medium heat for 2 minutes, being careful not to brown them. Add the cherry tomatoes and reduce to a low heat, cooking them for 5 minutes until softened.

Meanwhile, in a separate pan, heat the vermouth gently over a low heat with the chilli powder. Pour this into the tomato mixture.

Turn the heat up to medium-high. Add the fresh and tinned clams to the mixture, give the whole thing a good stir and steam with the lid on the pan for 5 minutes or until all the shell-on clams have opened. Stir half way through. Once done, discard any clams that haven't opened.

Drain the pasta. Add the crème fraiche, if using, to the pasta and stir well. Otherwise, stir in the olive oil.

Add the clams to the pasta and stir through thoroughly, ensuring hot throughout.

Season to taste, sprinkle the parsley over the dish and serve with crusty bread.

Difficulty: ● ● ● ○ ○
Preparation time: 20 mins
Cooking time: 20 mins

Serving: 3-4

Storage: Eat immediately. Not suitable for reheating.

Recipe from **Kirstie**

Kirstie is an accounts clerk and
lives with her fiancé Zubher.

South Indian prawn curry

We both love curries and this is our quick
and easy Saturday night meal in! Enjoy.

Ingredients

2 red chillies, deseeded and sliced
1 red onion, chopped
2cm of root ginger, peeled and finely chopped
2-3 cloves of garlic, crushed
1 tbsp olive oil
1 tsp black mustard seeds
½ tsp fenugreek seeds
12 curry leaves
½ tsp cracked black peppercorns
½ tsp turmeric
150ml coconut milk
250g raw tiger prawns, or cooked & peeled prawns
Handful of fresh coriander, chopped
Salt and pepper
Lime wedges

Method

Put the chillies, onion, ginger and garlic into a food processor with 3-4 tablespoons of water and blitz into a paste. Set aside.

Heat the oil in a frying pan until hot. When almost smoking, add the mustard seeds, fenugreek seeds and curry leaves and fry for 10 seconds – the mustard seeds will pop! Reduce the heat and add the chilli, onion, ginger and garlic paste.

Cook without colouring for around 5 minutes, adding a little water if necessary or if the mixture begins to stick. Stir in the cracked peppercorns and turmeric then stir in the coconut milk. Add the prawns to the mixture and cook through for a few minutes until completely pink.

Season to taste. Squeeze the lime over the curry and top with the fresh coriander.

Serve with basmati rice or warm chapatis.

Difficulty: ●●○○○
Preparation time: 20 mins
Cooking time: 20 mins

Serving: 2

176

Storage: Best eaten fresh.

Recipe by **Nicola Thomas**

Nicola is a full-time mum and lives in Bishopston
with her husband and two vehicle-mad boys.
She likes to meal plan and use up leftovers.

Prawn saganaki

This recipe is a favourite of my dad's. Reading the books of Lawrence and Gerald Durrell, he developed a passion for the island of Corfu. Many fantastic holidays have been spent in the area, drinking wine by the sea in Kalami bay, and eating this fantastic but simple recipe. Over the years it's been Anglicised a bit but that feeling of being on holiday remains.

Ingredients

1 tbsp extra virgin olive oil
1 onion, chopped
1 clove of garlic, crushed
400g tin of peeled plum tomatoes or a large handful of fresh tomatoes, roughly chopped
1 tbsp tomato purée
Good pinch of sugar
A splash of Ouzo, or 1 tsp crushed fennel seeds
100g Feta cheese, cubed
12 black olives, pitted
Handful of fresh parsley, chopped
200g cooked shell-on tiger prawns

Method

Heat the oil in a medium saucepan and sauté the onion and garlic (and fennel seeds, if using) over a medium heat for around 4 minutes until soft and translucent. Add the tomatoes and the tomato purée, then stir in the sugar. Reduce the heat and allow to simmer for around 15 minutes, adding a drizzle of water if the sauce thickens too much. Add the Ouzo (if using) then stir and continue to cook for a further 2-3 minutes.

Stir in the feta cheese, olives and parsley and then pile the prawns on top of the sauce. Continue to cook for 3-4 minutes more or until the prawns have warmed through.

Serve with rice or pasta, green salad, crusty bread to soak up the sauce and a glass of chilled white wine.

Difficulty: ● ● ○ ○ ○
Preparation time: 5 mins
Cooking time: 25-30 mins

Serving: 2

Storage: Best eaten fresh.

102 Cookery School

102 Gloucester Road, Bristol BS7 8BN
www.102cookeryschool.co.uk

Serving the local community with handy classes and workshops in all things culinary is **102 Cookery School** – a business started in June 2012 by Ben and Peter Gilks as a branch of their already award-winning family business, Nailsea Electrical.

Set in a beautiful converted church on the corner of Berkeley Road, the school holds 'demonstration and dine' evenings with Michelin-starred chefs as well as hands-on courses in everything from knife skills to foraging and sushi-making. 102 is also a popular choice for team building outings and hen parties and they even hold classes for the little ones.

Having been on Gloucester Road since the 80s, Nailsea Electrical are a permanent fixture and love to support other local businesses surrounding them, buying ingredients for their classes at 102 from their neighbours. Our very own Joe's Bakery even run their bread-making course!

Interior images © 102 Cookery School

Roast cod, brown shrimps and green sauce

This special roast fillet of cod with brown shrimps, green sauce, charred broccoli and oven dried tomatoes is sure to impress. Written by Nathan Muir for 102 Cookery School.

Ingredients

10 cherry tomatoes

Half a broccoli head

10 parsley leaves

5 mint leaves

5 basil leaves

15 blades of tarragon

2-3 anchovy fillets, chopped

1 tbsp capers

A handful of baby spinach leaves, chopped

1 clove of garlic, crushed

1 tsp of dijon mustard

100ml olive oil

3 drops of tabasco sauce

Juice of half a lemon juice

2 x 160g pieces of cod

Salt and pepper

Large knob of butter (around 10g)

100g brown shrimps

Method

Prepare the oven dried tomatoes in advance:
Preheat the oven to 140ºC. Bring a small pan of water to the boil. Score each tomato with a tiny cross on the bottom, blanch in the boiling water for about 30 seconds then remove with a slotted spoon and cool in a separate pan of iced water. When the tomatoes are cool enough to handle, remove the skins (they should peel off easily) and place them on a lined baking tray, season and bake for an hour.

To prepare the charred broccoli: Blanch the florets in boiling water for 1 minute and refresh in iced water (as with the tomatoes). Blot the blanched florets on a piece of kitchen towel. Heat a ribbed griddle pan, dress the broccoli in a little olive oil and cook for a few minutes until browned. Set aside.

To prepare the green sauce: Finely chop all the herbs together. Add the anchovies, capers, herbs, spinach and garlic to a bowl and mix with the dijon mustard, olive oil, tabasco and a squeeze of lemon juice and season well.

For the cod: Preheat oven to 180ºC.

Add a little olive oil to a non-stick pan and place over a medium heat. Dry the cod skin with a piece of kitchen towel. Place the cod skin side down into the hot pan and apply a little pressure to hold the skin flat. Fry gently for around 2 minutes until the skin crisps up. Place in the oven for around 5 minutes, or until cod is cooked through.

Remove from the oven, put the fish back in the pan over a low heat, add the butter and remaining lemon juice and baste. Add the brown shrimps, tomatoes and broccoli. Spoon over the butter to baste all ingredients and season with salt and pepper.

Serve the dish with the green sauce and warm new potatoes.

Difficulty: ● ● ● ● ○
Preparation time: 20 mins
Cooking time: 10 mins plus 1 hour for tomatoes

Serving: 2

Storage: Best eaten fresh.

Recipe by **Christine Higgs**

Loud Australian living with very quiet
English husband and two kids in Bishopston.
Quite impressed with Bristol life!

Homemade pizzas

This is one for the whole family. Get the kids involved making their own; and adults love it too. Our family favourite is margherita with Dave Giles' ham. The sauce can be made in advance and is enough for two large pizzas.

For the pizza base

15g fresh yeast (or a sachet of easy blend yeast)

2 tsp sugar or honey

250ml warm water

350g strong white bread flour

½ tsp salt

30ml olive oil

For rich tomato sauce

400ml passata

1 clove of garlic, crushed

A drizzle of olive oil

A few sprigs of oregano, finely chopped

TOP TIP

Use the base to make garlic pizza bread. Mix 50g butter with 2 crushed garlic cloves and 1 tbsp finely chopped parsley for the topping.

Method

To make the pizza dough, dissolve the yeast and sugar in the warm water. Leave for 10 minutes until frothy.

Put the flour and salt into a large mixing bowl, mix and make a well in the centre. Pour in the yeast mixture and the olive oil and mix well until it comes together into a ball.

Knead the dough on a clean, floured work surface for a good 10 minutes. Place the dough in an oiled bowl, cover with a damp tea towel and leave to rise for between 1-3 hours until it has doubled in size.

To prepare the tomato sauce, add all the ingredients to a saucepan and cook over a medium heat until at a gentle simmering point. Simmer for 10-15 minutes to reduce and thicken. Leave to cool.

Roll out the dough to preferred thickness on a clean, lightly floured surface and transfer to a large greased baking sheet, or two smaller baking sheets.

Toppings are limitless but here are a few ideas (quantities based on 1 large pizza):

For a simple margherita: Spread 150ml tomato sauce onto the base and top with 100g grated mozzarella and a few basil leaves.

Chicken and pesto: Spread the base with 2 tbsp pesto and top with strips of cooked chicken and cubes of mozzarella.

Difficulty: ● ● ● ○ ○
Preparation time:
35 mins (plus rising time)
Cooking time: 20 mins

Serving: Makes 2 large pizzas

Storage: Can be eaten cold the next day or reheated but best eaten fresh.

Recipe by
Sarah Newman

Sarah works in publishing
and likes mint ice cream,
being tidy and making
artwork out of paper.

Grandma Bimmy's cheese & onion quiche

V

Grandma Bimmy was a no-nonsense cook (and WI member) who specialised in simple, yet delicious food. This was one of my dad's favourite meals when he was growing up and now it's one of mine.

Ingredients

1 medium onion, finely chopped

300ml milk

225g plain flour

Pinch of salt

110g chilled butter, chopped into cubes

2–3 tbsp cold water

250g mature cheddar, grated

Black pepper

4 medium eggs, beaten

Difficulty: ● ● ○ ○ ○
Preparation time: 45 mins
Cooking time: 45 mins

Serving: 8

Storage: Store in an airtight container in the fridge for up to three days.

Method

Preheat oven to 180°C. Grease a flan tin of approximately 22cm in diameter.

Put the onions in a saucepan and cover with the milk. Place the saucepan over a low heat and simmer for 8-10 minutes, until the onions are softened. Strain the onions and discard the milk.

Sift the flour into a bowl with the salt. Add the butter and rub into the dry ingredients using your fingertips until the mixture resembles fine breadcrumbs (this can be done in a food processor). Gradually add the water and combine until the pastry holds together and can be made into a smooth ball. Handle as little as possible to avoid making the dough too sticky. Wrap in cling film and rest in the fridge for 30 minutes.

Lightly dust a clean surface with flour and roll out the dough until approximately 3mm thick – the pastry will need to hang over the edges of the tin to allow for shrinkage when baking.

Use the rolling pin to lift the pastry onto the tin so that it doesn't tear. Gently press into the tin and cut off the excess pastry.

Sprinkle the cheese into the bottom of the pastry case before adding the onions and the beaten egg, mixing round gently. Season to taste.

Cook in the oven for 45 minutes, or until nicely browned on top. A skewer inserted in the middle should come out clean.

Serve warm with new potatoes and salad, or cold in a lunchbox or with a picnic lunch.

Kookoo

429 Gloucester Road BS7 8TZ
www.kookoocafebristol.co.uk

Bringing authentic Persian cuisine to the heart of Gloucester Road is **Kookoo Cafe**, a new cafe/restaurant run by Moh and Christien and their lovely team. The venture began as a supper club of sorts with two evenings a week in Moh's brother's cafe, but popularity and a subscription list of over 200 people quickly called for a more permanent offering for Bristol's Iranian food lovers.

In early 2012 the couple opened Kookoo Cafe as an 'eat' cafe with only a few menu options per sitting, but this soon grew to include lunch specials and Sunday kebabs. Now the couple are opening a second, much bigger restaurant on nearby Filton Avenue so they no longer have to disappoint hungry customers at the weekends!

The concept, which they initially imagined would attract Bristol's Iranian community, has actually attracted a much wider fanbase with Persian food lovers from all over the world stopping by to enjoy Kookoo's warm hospitality. "We're informal and we like people to bring their friends. We enjoy looking after people!" says Christien. "There is so much misunderstanding about migrant communities that it's lovely that people are coming by and want to learn something about a different culture that they may not know much about."

Kookoo sabzi

Ⓥ

Ⓓ

This Persian dish is a form of omelette, which is usually baked in the oven. It is eaten all over the former Persian empire and has a huge variety of fillings. In Kookoo Café the dish is their trademark and they serve two vegetarian varieties: Kookoo sabzi (with green herbs) and Kookoo sib zamini (with potato).

Ingredients

1 tbsp sunflower oil

7 eggs

500g fresh green herbs stalks removed, chopped (including parsley, coriander, dill and chives)

Salt and pepper

¼ tsp turmeric

Barberries and walnuts (optional)

Method

Preheat oven to 200ºC.

Using an oven-safe 12 inch frying pan with a metal handle (or a similar sized deep baking tray) heat the oil in the oven, removing it before it starts to smoke.

Beat the eggs with the chopped herbs, salt and pepper and spices (and the barberries and walnuts if using). Pour the mixture into the pan, cover with aluminium foil and return to the oven for 20 minutes until the eggs are cooked. Remove the foil for the last five minutes of cooking to allow the Kookoo to brown on top.

Cut into pieces and serve with warm flatbread or pitta with salad and gherkins.

Difficulty: ●●○○○
Preparation time: 10 mins
Cooking time: 20 mins

Serving: 8

Storage: Best eaten fresh but after cooling, the Kookoo can be stored in the fridge for up to two days and can be eaten cold or reheated.

Recipe inspired by
Sarah Faunce

Sarah is an actuary. She likes cats
and dancing The Charleston.

Black-eyed bean casserole

Here's my recipe for black-eyed bean casserole.
I like this recipe because it's really healthy,
easy to make and tastes great!

Ingredients

1 tbsp olive oil

1 small onion, sliced

2 cloves of garlic, crushed

1 tsp coriander seeds, crushed

1 tsp cumin seeds, crushed

1 dried red chilli, deseeded and finely chopped

150g chestnut mushrooms, sliced

2 x 400g tins of cooked black-eyed beans, drained and rinsed

400g tin of chopped tomatoes

1 tbsp tomato purée

500ml vegetable or chicken stock

Salt and pepper

Handful of fresh coriander, roughly chopped

Method

Heat the oil in a saucepan and fry the onion for 2 minutes over a medium heat. Add the garlic, coriander, cumin and chilli and sauté for a few minutes until softened, stirring frequently to prevent it sticking to the pan. Add the mushrooms and sauté for another couple of minutes, mixing together well.

Stir in the black-eyed beans, tomatoes, tomato purée and stock. Simmer over a low heat for around 30 minutes or until reduced by a quarter. Season to taste and stir in the coriander just before serving.

Serve with long grain rice and an optional dollop of sour cream.

Difficulty: ●●○○○
Preparation time: 10 mins
Cooking time: 35-40 mins

Serving: 4

176

Storage: Will keep in fridge for three days. Suitable for freezing, use within a month and reheat thoroughly.

Recipe inspired by
Sue Pickering

Sue likes singing, dancing and making stuff. She lives in Westbury Park with her partner and two children.

Roast peppers & Mediterranean couscous

V

Sue Pickering's fantastic Mediterranean couscous recipe goes perfectly with these roast peppers to provide a filling veggie meal.

Ingredients

4 red peppers, de-seeded and halved lengthways (keep the stalk on)

4 tbsp olive oil

3 cloves of garlic, peeled and chopped

1 red onion, chopped

1 aubergine, cut into 2cm chunks

1 courgette, cut into 2cm chunks

150g cherry tomatoes, halved

180g couscous

360ml vegetable stock

Juice of a lemon

125g goats cheese

Salt and pepper

Fresh basil and toasted pine nuts to garnish

Method

Preheat oven to 200°C.

Lay the pepper halves cut side facing upwards on a baking tray, drizzle with olive oil and set aside.

Put two tablespoons of the olive oil into a large bowl. Add the garlic, onions, aubergine and courgette and toss the vegetables until well coated. Pour into a roasting tin, place in the oven and roast for 30 minutes, stirring half way through and adding the tomatoes to the roasting tin at this point. For the final 15 minutes, add the pepper halves to the oven too.

Meanwhile, put the couscous into a large bowl. Pour over the hot vegetable stock, the last tablespoon of olive oil and the lemon juice. Mix and cover the bowl with a plate or a sheet of cling film and leave for at least 10 minutes. Once the couscous has absorbed the stock, fluff up the grains with a fork to separate.

Add the couscous to the roasting tin and stir into the roasted vegetables. Season to taste.

Spoon the mixture into each pepper half and crumble the goats cheese over them. Then put all the stuffed peppers onto a baking tray and put back into the oven for 10 minutes to heat up and for the goats cheese to melt a little and brown.

To serve, place two peppers onto each plate. Add some fresh basil and some toasted pine nuts to garnish. Serve with a green salad.

Difficulty: ● ● ● ○ ○
Preparation time: 20 mins
Cooking time: 40 mins

Serving: 4

Storage: Keep in fridge and eat within two days. Reheat thoroughly. Not suitable for freezing.

Harvest

11 Gloucester Road BS7 8AA

www.harvest-bristol.coop

PENNE PASTA
LOOSE (ORG)
ESSENTIAL

£2.40/kg

GREEN LENTILS
(ORG)

£3.90/kg

CHICK PEAS

£2.6

As part of Essential Trading, a leading UK organic and fairtrade wholesaler, **Harvest** have been part of Gloucester Road for 15 years but have traded as a health food shop since way back in 1971. "We love Gloucester Road," says Anne-Marie, Harvest's co-op member (acting manager).

"It's brimming with personality and has a great community atmosphere."

As the only fully vegan and vegetarian food store in Bristol, Harvest sell everything from dried foods, cereals and pulses to herbal teas, organic fruit and veg, speciality bread and raw foods.

Their deli counter is packed with raw chocolate brownies amongst other vegetarian and vegan sweet and savoury treats, and they even stock cruelty-free body care products and refills for eco-friendly cleaning products. A true one stop shop for all things environmentally friendly.

Pesto & butter bean burgers

V

These versatile burgers can be tweaked to make them dairy-free if using vegan pesto, and gluten-free by swapping the breadcrumbs and buns for gluten-free alternatives, all available from Harvest.

Ingredients

2 x 400g tins of butter beans, drained and rinsed

3 tbsp red pesto

115g wholemeal breadcrumbs

1 clove of garlic, crushed

1 red onion, finely diced

Salt and pepper

Squeeze of lemon

Method

Preheat oven to 200ºC.

Place the beans and pesto in a food processor and blend until you have a chunky paste. Add the breadcrumbs, garlic and onion to the paste and stir in to combine. Season with salt, pepper and a squeeze of lemon.

Using damp hands, shape the mixture into eight burgers. Place on a lined or greased baking tray. Bake in the oven for 30-40 minutes until golden brown.

Serve in wholemeal buns with sliced tomato and salad leaves.

TOP TIP

Whisk together 2 tablespoons of olive oil, 2 tablespoons of flaxseed oil and 2 tablespoons of pesto as a great way to boost your omega 3 fatty acids intake. This mixture can be used as a healthy dressing in a salad or to drizzle over vegetables and will keep in the fridge for 2-3 days.

Difficulty: ●●○○○
Preparation time: 15 mins
Cooking time: 40 mins

Serving: Makes 8 burgers

Storage: Will keep uncooked in fridge for two days. Suitable for freezing before cooking, use within a month and reheat thoroughly.

Recipe by **Kerry** at **Bishopston Matters**

Kerry is the editor of Bishopston Matters and a keen vegetarian.

Glamorgan sausages

Ⓥ

If you are cooking either sausage and mash or a roast dinner, these yummy sausages allow us veggies to have all the same trimmings rather than a completely different meal. They are also a real hit with non-vegetarians.

Ingredients

1 small onion, finely diced

Knob of butter

250g breadcrumbs

170g strong cheddar, grated

3-4 tbsp flat leaf parsley, finely chopped

1 heaped tsp of mustard powder

Salt and pepper

4 eggs

50g plain flour for dusting

Sunflower oil

Method

Sweat the diced onion in a little butter over a medium heat for 2-3 minutes until softened slightly. Mix 170g of the breadcrumbs with the onion, cheese, flat leaf parsley, mustard powder and salt and pepper in a large bowl. Beat three of the eggs in a small bowl and add this to the mixture, combining well.

Dampen your hands and roll the mixture into 10/12 sausage shapes, about a handful for each sausage.

Tip the flour onto a plate and season. Beat the remaining egg and pour onto a second plate and tip the remaining breadcrumbs onto a third. Roll each sausage in seasoned flour, then in the beaten egg and finally coat with the breadcrumbs.

Heat the oil in a large frying pan and shallow fry the sausages over a medium heat for 12-15 minutes, turning occasionally until golden brown.

Serve with mustard mash, garlic-tossed savoy cabbage and onion gravy or as part of a veggie roast.

TOP TIP

At Christmas, add cranberries and goats cheese to make a lovely seasonal meal.

Difficulty: ●●●○○
Preparation time: 40 mins
Cooking time: 15 mins

Serving: Makes 10-12 sausages

Storage: The mixture can be frozen at the point before you add beaten egg and roll in breadcrumbs.

Recipe by **Jemima Lumley**

Jemima is a full-time jeweller and
part-time craftsperson with a
houseful of unfinished projects.

SLOW COOKED

Red cabbage with apples

V
Vg
D

Here is a family recipe for red cabbage. Best cooked the day before, this recipe will win over red cabbage haters! I know as I have achieved this on several occasions.

Ingredients

2 tbsp extra virgin olive oil

1 large onion, finely sliced

2 tbsp caster sugar

1 red cabbage cut into quarters, centre removed and finely sliced

2 large cooking apples, peeled, cored and diced

100g sultanas

Salt and pepper

½ nutmeg, grated

300ml vegetable or chicken stock

3 tbsp balsamic vinegar

Method

Heat the oil in a very large pan. Add the onion and cook over a medium heat until softened, for around five minutes. Sprinkle in the sugar and stir until the onions are golden and beginning to caramelise. Stir in the cabbage, apples and sultanas. Season well with salt and pepper before adding the nutmeg. Pour over the stock and the balsamic vinegar, cover and leave to cook over a low heat for 2 hours, stirring occasionally.

Serve with roasted meats and game or with cold meats and cheese.

TOP TIP

Leftovers in our house are eaten the following day in a sandwich with cream cheese, on top of some scrambled eggs. Even my fussy teenager will eat that for weekend brunch!

Difficulty: ●●○○○
Preparation time: 25 mins
Cooking time: 2½ hours

Serving: 8-12 as a side dish

Storage: Keep covered in fridge and use within three days. Can be eaten cold. Suitable for freezing, defrost and reheat thoroughly.

Gardner's Patch

159 Gloucester Road BS7 8BA

www.gardnerspatch.co.uk

Fresh is Best Naturally

ENG CUCUMBERS 89P EACH

Class:

Providing the people of Gloucester Road with quality fruit and veg is **Gardner's Patch**, a family-run business for the last 25 years. With a second branch in Weston-super-Mare and a third open in 2013.

With a friendly team of staff dedicated to bringing the freshest seasonal produce to the locals, you can buy the everyday to the most exotic here, from potatoes and carrots to lime leaves and aubergines. There is always a great selection of herbs and you'll even find free-range eggs, homemade preserves and Bishopston honey on sale.

As a Bristol Pound business, you can use TXT2PAY to pay for your groceries at Gardner's Patch, supporting the local economy along the way. "We offer something to the customers that supermarkets can't," says Nicole Vinton. "Guaranteed fresh, locally grown, quality produce at great prices. You can't beat having the freshest seasonal produce all year round."

Wintergold stew

This vegetarian stew from Gardner's Patch makes the most of fresh produce. A warming autumnal dish, best enjoyed with crusty bread and butter.

Ingredients

1 tbsp vegetable oil

1 onion, peeled and diced

2 sticks of celery, chopped

1 red pepper, deseeded and chopped

4 cloves of garlic, crushed

1 litre vegetable or chicken stock

1 butternut squash, peeled and diced

2 sweet potatoes, peeled and diced

3 tsp chopped fresh oregano or thyme

1½ tsp paprika

1 tsp salt

½ tsp ground black pepper

Large handful of kale, chopped

Small bunch of parsley, chopped

Method

Heat the oil in a large saucepan. Add the onion, celery, red pepper and garlic and sauté for around 5 minutes.

Add the stock, squash, sweet potato, oregano, paprika, salt and pepper and bring to a simmer. Cook for 30 to 40 minutes over a low to medium heat until the sweet potato is tender, stirring occasionally. Stir in the kale and cook for a further 10 minutes.

To thicken, mash the squash and sweet potato against the side of the pan with the back of a spoon. Stir in the parsley and allow the stew to stand for 5-10 minutes before serving.

Adjust seasoning to taste.

Ladle into bowls and serve hot with fresh bread and butter.

Difficulty: ●○○○○
Preparation time: 10 mins
Cooking time: 1 hour

Serving: 4-6

Storage: Keep covered in fridge and use within three days. Suitable for freezing. Reheat thoroughly.

Sweet things

Playfull Toyshop

87 Gloucester Road BS7 8AS

Playfull Toyshop is run by local couple Kerstin and Nigel Price who began their Gloucester Road residency back in 2002 when Kerstin sold cloth dolls and wooden toys from the upstairs room at number 87. Two years later when the main shop became vacant, they took the plunge, moved downstairs and never looked back.

Selling a huge range of toys, games, books and arts and crafts for children from birth to around the age of 12, they ensure that everything they stock is made from sustainably sourced materials like rubber and wood.

Having lived in the area for 33 years, Kerstin and Nigel were customers on Gloucester Road way before they became shopkeepers and their favourite thing about it is the real feeling of community and togetherness that it has to offer. "We can't imagine being anywhere else," they say proudly.

ℒ

Swedish Sunday Cake

Kerstin at Playfull Toyshop has shared
this traditional Swedish recipe which has
a gorgeous gooey caramel topping.

For the cake base

150g butter, room temperature

130g caster sugar

1 medium egg, beaten

1 tsp baking powder

300g plain flour

For the topping

100g butter

100g caster sugar

100g flaked almonds

2 tsp vanilla extract

2 tbsp double cream

Method

Preheat oven to 200ºC. Grease and line a round 18cm spring-form cake tin.

To prepare the base, cream the butter and sugar in a large mixing bowl. Add the egg and mix well. Sift the baking powder with the flour into the cake mixture and combine thoroughly. Gather together with your hands into a soft ball. The consistency will be similar to shortbread dough.

Cover the dough with cling film and chill for 10 minutes.

Meanwhile, prepare the topping. Place the butter and sugar in a pan and place over a low heat. Once the butter has melted and the sugar dissolved, add the almonds, vanilla extract and the cream, stirring well. Increase the heat slightly and cook for 3-4 minutes until the colour of the mixture is a light honey brown, stirring constantly as the mixture can burn easily. Remove from the heat.

Remove the dough from the fridge. Reserving a small amount of pastry to make a lattice pattern for the top of the cake, place the rest of the dough inside the cake tin and pat out evenly. Pour the topping from the pan evenly over the dough. With the remaining dough, cut 6 strips and lay them across the topping, three going horizontally and three vertically to create a lattice effect.

Bake for 25-30 min until the cake is a light golden brown colour. Remove from the oven and allow to cool completely before removing from the tin.

Delicious served alone or warmed with whipped cream or ice cream and fresh berries.

Difficulty: ● ● ● ○ ○
Preparation time: 30 mins
Cooking time: 30 mins

Serving: 8

Storage: Once cooled, keep in fridge and eat within three days. Can be warmed through in the oven.

Recipe by
Judy Gowenlock

Judy has lived in St Andrews for 20
years and enjoys sharing the delights of
Gloucester Road with family and friends.

Hilda's sticky gingerbread cake

Ⓥ

This recipe was made by my paternal grandmother, Hilda, who loved making cakes. She saved her sugar rations during the war in order to bake at the end of the week. It reminds me of my mum and her love of baking – she adapted it and regularly made it during my childhood.

Ingredients

225g plain flour

2 tsp ground ginger (add more for extra spice)

150ml milk

1 level tsp bicarbonate of soda

115g soft dark brown sugar

115g butter

225g black treacle

1 egg, beaten

Method

Preheat oven to 130ºC. Grease and line a 23cm square baking tin.

Sift the flour and ginger into a large mixing bowl.

Take a few teaspoons of the milk and mix with bicarbonate of soda in a separate bowl.

Put the sugar, butter, treacle and the remaining milk in a saucepan and warm over a low heat until the butter has melted, stirring all the time to avoid burning. Remove from the heat. Carefully add the milk and bicarbonate of soda mixture.

Add this mixture slowly, in stages, to the flour and ginger, mixing well each time to remove any lumps. Add the beaten egg.

Pour the mixture into the prepared tin.

Bake for approximately 1 hour 10 minutes on the middle shelf of the oven until firm to the touch.

Allow to cool slightly before removing the gingerbread carefully from the tin, stripping off the greaseproof paper before it cools completely.

Difficulty: ●●○○○
Preparation time: 15 mins
Cooking time: 1 hour 15 mins

Serving: 16

Storage: Keeps for up to a week in a cake tin. Suitable for freezing, defrost thoroughly before eating.

Tart

16 The Promenade,
Gloucester Rd BS7 8AE
www.lovelytart.com

Feeling more akin to a French salon than an English cafe, **Tart** is Gloucester Road's answer to any of your afternoon tea or other cake-related needs.

Recently taken over by original head chef Andrew Griffin, Tart was first opened by a local family four and a half years ago and has built up a reputation for providing the residents of Bishopston, Cotham and Redland with exceptional food.

This includes an impressive breakfast menu, the most delicious pancakes you'll ever eat, their namesake savoury tarts come lunchtime, there is then a whole selection of afternoon tea options. Tart have even begun rolling out their 'Tart After Dark' evenings on a weekly basis and now open on Friday and Saturday evenings too. With a weekly changing menu of seasonal delights made from produce

bought locally, Andrew is pleased with the success of his business and is glad to be part of such a diverse area as Gloucester Road. "Everybody seems to get on with everyone else," he says. "There's no ridiculous business rivalries. Everybody wants everybody to do well and succeed." With a reputation that precedes them and a selection of cakes that can't be beaten for miles, Tart are definitely in it for the long haul.

Tunisian orange cake

This is possibly the quickest and easiest
cake ever to make! It's so tasty and moist
and is one of our best sellers at Tart.

For the cake

200g caster sugar
100g ground almonds
60g breadcrumbs
1 ½ tsp baking powder
200ml vegetable oil
4 medium eggs
Zest of 1 large orange
Zest of 1 small lemon

For the syrup

85g caster sugar
1 large or 2 small
cinnamon sticks
Juice from the above
orange and lemon
3 or 4 star anise
7 or 8 cloves

Method

Preheat oven to 160ºC. Grease and line a
round 20cm cake tin.

Pour all of the cake ingredients into a bowl
and mix well until combined. Pour into the
lined cake tin and bake for around 45 minutes.
The cake is cooked when a skewer inserted in
the centre comes out clean.

To make the syrup, pour the juice from the
orange and lemon into a small saucepan.
Add the sugar and spices and cook over a
medium heat for around 10 minutes until the
ingredients have reduced to a sticky syrup.

Allow to cool slightly then pour the syrup over
the cake. The spices can be removed with a
sieve before the syrup is poured or can be left
on for decoration.

Difficulty: ● ● ○ ○ ○
Preparation time: 15 mins
Cooking time: 45 mins

Serving: 8

Storage: Keep in an airtight
container and consume within
a week.

Recipe by
Catriona Irvine

Catriona is a play therapist and
qualified beekeeper.

Granny's chocolate pudding

V

D

This is an easy, traditional, self-saucing pudding my granny used to make when I was young. Great served smothered with thick cream or ice cream.

Ingredients

115g butter or margarine
115g caster sugar
2 eggs
1 tsp vanilla essence
2 level tbsp cocoa powder
85g self raising flour

For the sauce

115g soft brown sugar
2 level tbsp cocoa powder
285ml hot water

Method

Preheat oven to 190ºC.
Grease a deep ovenproof dish.

Cream butter and sugar together in a large mixing bowl. Beat in the eggs one at a time then stir in the vanilla essence. Fold in the cocoa powder and flour and mix until completely combined.

Pour mixture into the prepared dish.

Mix together the sauce ingredients in a jug and stir well until the sugar dissolves before pouring over the top of the cake mixture.

Bake for 40 minutes. If the cake is ready, a skewer inserted into the centre should come out clean apart from the sauce which should be bubbling around the top of the cake.

Difficulty: ● ● ○ ○ ○
Preparation time: 10 mins
Cooking time: 40 mins

Serving: 6

Storage: Once cooled, keep in fridge and eat within two days. Reheat or can be eaten cold.

Recipe by **Ruth Proctor**

Ruth is a freelance German and Russian
translator. She lives in Bedminster.

Chocolate fridge cake

V

Super quick, super easy and super
tasty! This chocolate fridge cake is a
bit like tiffin without the fuss.

Ingredients

100g butter

1 tbsp soft light
brown sugar

2 tbsp golden syrup

3 tbsp cocoa powder

200g milk or
dark chocolate

200g Rich Tea or
digestive biscuits

50g sultanas, dried
apricots or chopped
hazelnuts

Method

Line a 20cm square shallow tin with
greaseproof paper.

Add the butter, sugar, golden syrup and cocoa
to a saucepan and melt over a low heat.

Meanwhile, bring a separate saucepan of
water to a gentle simmer and place the
chocolate in a bowl over the top, stirring
until the chocolate has melted.

Break the biscuits into small pieces and stir
into the melted butter mixture along with the
sultanas, apricots or hazelnuts until everything
is coated well.

Pour this mixture into the prepared tin and
spread out evenly.

Spread the melted chocolate over the top
before placing the tin in the fridge to set.
This should take around 90 minutes.

Cut into 12 fingers to serve or just break
into pieces.

Difficulty: ●○○○○
Preparation time: 10 mins
Cooking time: 15 mins. Plus up
to 3 hours to set in the fridge.

Serving: 12

Storage: Best kept in the fridge.
Will keep for up to two weeks.

Scrumptiously Sweet

83 Gloucester Road BS7 8AS
www.scrumptiouslysweet.co.uk

A traditional high street just wouldn't be right without a sweet shop and in 2008 Gloucester Road acquired its very own. Filled with a huge range of sweets and confectionary including a range of pick 'n' mix to delight any child and nostalgic treats for the adults, **Scrumptiously Sweet** even offers a great range of sugar-free and vegetarian products so that nobody needs to miss out. The shop also stocks a beautiful array of belgian chocolates which are perfect for that special gift.

In the last 18 months, owner Melonie Telfer and her team have extended their offer to include a new range of bakeware and cake decorating equipment in a separate area to the rear of the shop. From ready-to-roll icing to cake glitter and muffin cases, they even have cake tins available to hire to would-be cake bakers. The sweet-lovers needn't worry as their baking range grows however as Melonie reassures us. "We'll never give up our sweets, the kids will wonder what's happening!" So whether it's jelly beans or coconut ice, sugar paste or cake tins you're after, Scrumptiously Sweet is your place.

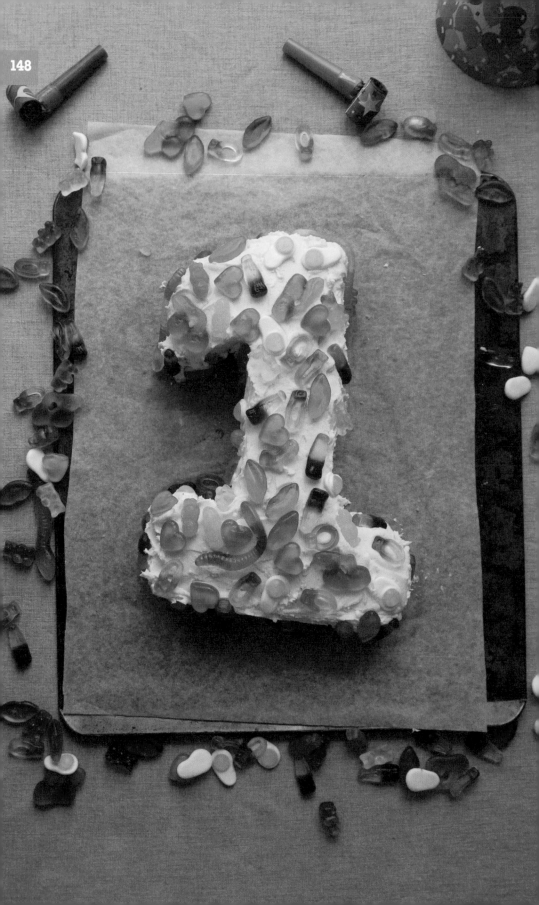

Birthday sponge cake

Scrumptiously Sweet hire out all sorts of cake tins for birthdays and celebrations. This is the recipe they recommend to use for them.

For the cake

225g unsalted butter, softened
225g golden caster sugar
4 large eggs, beaten
1 tsp vanilla extract
225g self raising flour
2 tsp baking powder

For the icing

140g butter, softened
280g icing sugar
1½ to 2½ tsp lemon extract (optional)

Method

Preheat oven to 180°C. Grease your cake tin, or use cake release spray. Double line the tin on the outside with foil or baking paper and place on a baking tray.

Cream together the butter and caster sugar. Beat in the egg, a little at a time. Add the vanilla extract.

Sift the flour and baking powder into the mixture and fold in with a metal spoon until thoroughly combined, remembering to scrape any cake mixture from the sides of the bowl.

Spoon the mixture into the prepared cake tin and place on the centre shelf of the oven. Bake for 25-35 minutes, until well risen and golden in colour. Remove from the oven, leave in the tin for 5-10 minutes to cool before transferring to a cooling rack.

To prepare the icing, put the butter and icing sugar in a large bowl. Mix together with a fork, adding the lemon extract a little at time to taste. Spread on to the cooled cake. This should be enough to cover the top and sides.

Decorate with your choice of sweets.

Difficulty: ●●○○○
Preparation time: 20 mins
Cooking time: 40 mins

Serving: 12

Storage: Will keep in a tin or sealed container for up to one week. If it lasts that long!

Recipe by
Margaret Debley

My favourite occupation is being
a grandma. Also a professional
musician living in Redland.

Mincemeat upside-down pudding

V

This is an old family recipe from the 1940s. It has a fabulous festive flavour thanks to the mincemeat.

Ingredients

60g self raising flour
60g caster sugar
40g butter
1 level tsp baking powder
1 level tsp mixed spice
1 egg
Pinch of salt
2 tsp cold water
100g mincemeat

Method

Preheat oven to 190ºC.

Place all ingredients except for the mincemeat in a bowl and beat together for one minute.

Grease a small ovenproof pudding dish (approximately 1 pint capacity) with butter, and add the mincemeat to the base. Pour the pudding mixture on top and level it out.

Cook for 25-30 minutes. When it's ready, a skewer should come out clean and the cake should be spongy and bounce back when lightly pressed.

Serve with custard, cream or brandy sauce.

Difficulty: ●●○○○
Preparation time: 10 mins
Cooking time: 30 mins

Serving: 4

Storage: Best eaten warm. Once cooled, keep in fridge and reheat within two days.

Recipe by
Hannah Lowery

Hannah lives in St Andrews
with O, F and S.

UNDER 30 MINS

Caramelised coconut rice pudding

A lovely quick pudding for easy entertaining.
This is a firm favourite with friends and family.

Ingredients

8 heaped tbsp arborio or pudding rice
300ml milk
300ml coconut milk
6 tbsp water
25g butter
4 tbsp caster sugar
1 tbsp demerara sugar

Method

Put the rice in a medium sized heavy-based pan and stir in the milk, coconut milk and water.

Bring to the boil over a medium heat, then reducing the heat to a simmer, cook for 15 to 20 minutes until the rice has swelled. Stir regularly. The rice should be soft but have a little bite.

Add the butter and stir in the caster sugar.

Spoon into a serving dish and sprinkle with demerara sugar. Glaze the top with a blowtorch or place under a hot grill, watching closely until the sugar has melted and turned golden.

Difficulty: ●●○○○
Preparation time: 5 mins
Cooking time: 20 mins

Serving: 4

Storage: Once cooled, keep covered in fridge for no more than two days. Reheat thoroughly.

Bristanbul

137 Gloucester Road BS7 8AX

www.bristanbul.co.uk

Tel: 0117 924 0003

OPEN

Lavash Flat Bread

(Eggless & Vegan)

£1.60

Bringing a taste of Turkey to Gloucester Road is **Bristanbul**, a Turkish bakery and patisserie selling a great range of savoury and sweet snacks. With everything from mouth-watering baklava to meringues, traditional puddings and flatbreads on offer, the family run business, which has been on the old Greggs site since April 2011, is the perfect place to pick up a last minute dessert on your way home or even a quick snack for lunch.

Everything is freshly made on the premises daily and as well as their range of yummy eastern treats, they stock an equally extensive range of the less unusual; from cheesecakes to cookies and even the odd gingerbread man! Also specialising in gluten-free desserts, Bristanbul have all bases covered.

"We love Gloucester Road," says Hulya Macil, Bristanbul's owner. "It's like a town of its own within Bristol, everyone's like family and all of the neighbouring businesses help each other out. We love it here!"

Keşkül

Ⓥ

This traditional, gluten-free, almond
based milk pudding is a popular dish
in Turkey, and at Bristanbul too!

Ingredients

40g corn starch

10 tbsp cold water

1 litre of milk

200g caster sugar

50g desiccated coconut

3 egg yolks

1 drop of vanilla extract

Method

Mix the corn starch with the water and stir well.

Add the milk, sugar, coconut, egg yolks and vanilla to a saucepan and cook over a medium heat, stirring constantly until just before it begins to boil. Mix in the corn starch mixture and stir until boiling.

Reduce the heat to low, add the vanilla and stir continuously for around 5 minutes until the mixture thickens slightly.

Pour the pudding, whilst hot, into separate portion dishes and allow to cool.

Once cooled, decorate with coconut and pistachio or ground walnuts. Serve cold.

Difficulty: ●○○○○
Preparation time: 5 mins
Cooking time: 15 mins

Serving: 4-6

Storage: Keep in the fridge and consume within two days.

Recipe by
Katie Skuse

Katie enjoys photography,
travel, food and spending
time on Gloucester Road.

Apple strudel

v

This is a recipe that my grandma used to make. She then passed the recipe to my aunt and then it was passed to me! I have fond memories of eating this at my grandparents' house when I was a child.

Ingredients

8 Granny Smith apples, peeled·and cored

Juice and zest of an unwaxed lemon

6 sheets of ready-made filo pastry

50g melted butter

200g breadcrumbs (as prepared on p176)

100g demerara sugar

2 tsp cinnamon

150g sultanas

Method

Cut the apples into wedges and grate, either by hand or in a food processor. Place into a bowl and squeeze over the lemon juice to prevent the apples from browning.

Unroll the filo sheets. On a floured surface, lay out one sheet horizontally. Then, to make the surface area larger lay another sheet above the first, so that the two long sides are overlapping by around 3cm. Brush some butter onto the overlapping area of the bottom sheet to stick the two sheets together.

Add a second layer of filo to make the base layer thicker. To do this, brush melted butter over the whole of the large filo layer. Then lay two more sheets on top of the first layer so that the whole surface is covered.

Add another coating of melted butter over the second filo layer. Then sprinkle half of each amount of the breadcrumbs, grated apples, demerara sugar, lemon zest, cinnamon and sultanas over the top.

Next, add another layer of filo on top of the apple layer by using two more sheets to cover the whole surface area. Once again, stick the two halves together by brushing the overlapping strip with butter. Then brush the whole surface area with butter and sprinkle over the remaining breadcrumbs followed by the apples, sugar, lemon zest, cinnamon and sultanas.

Fold the end and roll the strudel up gently. Place carefully on a baking tray and with a pastry brush cover with melted butter to stop the pastry from splitting when cooking.

Bake for 45-50 minutes. Don't worry if your strudel splits – when it cools the apple and sugar will make it set.

Leave to cool for 5-10 minutes and sprinkle with icing sugar. Cut into thick slices and eat warm with cream or ice cream.

Difficulty: ● ● ● ○ ○
Preparation time: 30 mins
Cooking time: 40 mins
. . . .
Serving: 10
. . . .
Storage: Keep covered in the fridge and eat within two days. Can be eaten cold or reheated.

Recipe by
Rima Bhattacharya

Rima lives in Bristol and teaches law.
She loves Indian food but has a major
aversion to coriander!

OVERNIGHTER

Shrikhand

Most Indian desserts are laden with clarified butter and sugar – not great after a curry. This dessert is different; sweet but light and the perfect end to a meal.

Ingredients

500g Greek yoghurt
250g caster sugar
½ tsp ground cardamom
Pinch of saffron
20g pistachios, chopped
20g almonds, chopped

Method

Mix together the yoghurt and sugar in a large bowl. Add the cardamom powder and saffron and stir in well. Reserving some of the chopped nuts for decorating at the end, add the rest of them to the yoghurt mixture and combine. Cover and chill in the fridge overnight.

Remove from the fridge and mix well. Divide the mixture into six bowls and sprinkle the remaining nuts over the shrikhand.

Serve with slices of fresh mango.

Difficulty: ●○○○○
Preparation time: Overnight
Cooking time: None

Serving: 6

Storage: Once prepared, keep in fridge and eat within two days.

The Family Practice

116 Gloucester Road BS7 8NL
www.thefamilypractice.tv

The Family Practice is a well respected osteopathic and complementary therapy centre that provides treatment and advice for a wide variety of health issues and injuries. They offer therapies such as accupuncture, homeopathy, nutritional advice, therapeutic massage, counselling and Alexander technique. aswell as osteopathic treatment.

Set up and run by the Hounsfield family, with a seperate satellite clinic in Southville, they offer expert care that is affordable for the whole family. Their Bristol Children's Clinic specialises in osteopathic care of children and newborn babies, and many of the practitioners also specialise in treatments for the expectant mother.

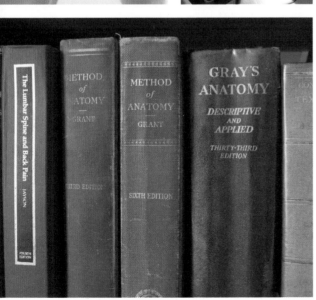

World's healthiest cookies

V **Vg** **D**

These cookies by Norma, the nutritionist at The Family Practice, are a half-way house between a flapjack and a traditional cookie. They are delicious and almost good for you!

Ingredients

2 very ripe bananas

2 tbsp olive oil

2 tbsp maple syrup

150g jumbo old fashioned oats (or gluten-free oats)

2 tbsp flaxseed or linseed

1 tsp cinnamon

½ tsp ground cardamom (4/5 pods if you grind your own)

3-4 dates, chopped

35g raisins

1 ½ tbsp fresh ginger, finely diced

4-5 walnuts, crushed

Method

Preheat oven to 170ºC.

In a large mixing bowl, mash the bananas until liquified. Add the olive oil and maple syrup and stir to combine. Add the oats, flaxseed, cinnamon and cardamom and combine well. Finally, mix in the dates, raisins, ginger and walnuts.

Spoon heaped tablespoonfuls of the mixture onto a non-stick or lined baking sheet and flatten out to your desired shape. The cookies will not change in size while cooking, so don't worry about putting them too close together.

Bake for 15-20 minutes, you'll be able to smell when they are almost ready.

Allow to cool on the tray for a few minutes before transferring to a wire rack to cool completely.

TOP TIP

To chop ginger finely put it in a mini food processor (or grate with the small blade on a cheese grater).

Difficulty: ●○○○○
Preparation time: 20 mins
Cooking time: 20 mins

Serving: 12 cookies

Storage: Store in an airtight container and consume within a week.

Recipe by
Charlotte Whitten
Charlotte lives in St Andrews with
her husband and two small boys and
has a very sweet tooth.

OVERNIGHTER

Nutty ice lollies

I love pistachio ice cream but you just can't buy it in tubs like all the other flavours. Now I have the next best thing on tap all year round. Bliss!

Ingredients

50g finely ground pistachios or ground almonds

1 tsp vanilla extract or 1 tsp almond extract if using ground almonds

60g caster sugar

60ml single cream

60ml fromage frais

225ml water

Method

Put all of the ingredients into a blender and blitz until everything is mixed well.

Using a fine sieve, strain the liquid into a jug. Place the pistachio residue into a small bowl and set aside – this can be eaten separately or discarded.

Pour the strained liquid into your favourite ice lolly moulds or ice cube trays and place in the freezer. Freeze overnight.

TOP TIP

Try using ready-made custard instead of fromage frais for a yummy alternative.

Difficulty: ●○○○○
Preparation time: 10 mins
Cooking time: None, although overnight for freezing.

Serving: 6-8 ice lollies

Storage: Keep in the freezer and consume within a month.

Extras

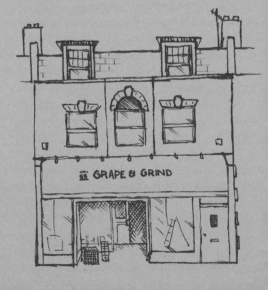

Grape & Grind

101 Gloucester Rd BS7 8AT
www.grapeandgrind.co.uk

After spotting a gap in the market and plenty of Saturday morning queues snaking their way through the doorways of Gloucester Road independents, husband and wife team Darren and Polly Willis were impressed with local loyalty and plumped for Bishopston as their new home and location of their dream business venture, a wine shop. And after relocating from London in November 2010 and opening the doors of **Grape & Grind**, they couldn't be happier with their choice.

With a huge selection of wines to please the palate of any connoisseur, Grape & Grind specialise in sourcing from smaller, independent producers and winemakers. But with a good mix of wines from all over the world and a great range of prices, even the post-work visit for a bottle of white to drink with friends is catered for.

With a great selection of spirits also available for the discerning lover of whisky, rum, gin and brandy, Darren and Polly have all bases covered. Even local cider, tea and coffee can be sourced here as well as a beautiful range of glassware. "Hopefully, for people who are interested in food and drink, there's something here for everyone," says Darren.

Perfect matches

Darren Willis from Grape & Grind has chosen some of the recipes from the book and found some fantastic wine matches. Here, he tells you what they are and why he's chosen them...

Moroccan lamb tagine

With a dish like tagine, I'm immediately thinking of deeply flavoured wines with warm fruit and a hint of spice. The **Calmel+JJoseph Cotes du Roussillon Villages 2011** has a deep ruby colour with a good intensity. The nose is rich and complex packed with red and black fruits followed by intense garrigue and spicy notes. The palate is well structured and full bodied with ripe tannins, offering an elegant and well balanced wine. At the recent International Wine Challenge tasting, this was the only wine from Languedoc or Roussillon given the top 'Trophy' award. It's certainly worth it.

South Indian prawn curry

Often a difficult match depending on the level of spice, and in this case we're using coconut milk, some chilli and many other aromatic spices. A wine that has a little extra richness works fantastically with dishes like this but I also think that really fresh acidity is important too. The **Two Rivers Riesling, Marlborough 2011** has opulent floral aromas with lime flower, lemon rind and tropical fruit. A ripe peach note and juicy acidity are paired with flickering minerality on the superbly balanced palate. A vibrant expression of pristine Riesling flavours, very pure with a long lingering finish.

Wild rabbit

Wine loves rabbit! It has a real depth of flavour compared with other white meat and a touch of gameyness that good wine works really well with. Perhaps unsurprisingly I've plumped for a Pinot Noir for this recipe, but what is unusual is that this one hails from Austria. The **Stift Goettweig Pinot Noir, Goettweiger 2011** could best be described as a cross between a mid-weight quality Central Otago Pinot and a good quality Burgundy. Full of fruit and savoury aromas and flavours with developing sweet tannins, fresh balanced acidity and a lingering finish whilst not overpowering the flavour of the rabbit.

p82

p98

p70

Hay-smoked mackerel

An oily fish marinated in vinegar requires a very specific style of wine. Preparing fish this way is very popular in Portugal and as we're looking for a crisp, dry white with vibrant acidity I would look no further than Vinho Verde. **Clip do Monte da Vaia Loureiro, Vinho Verde 2012**. The variety Loureiro makes some of the standout Vinho Verdes. This fruit-focused beauty is a clear expression of Loureiro. It's gently floral, with juicy flesh (succulent melon) and a mineral/citrus core. Ripe, round and fruity but refreshing and saltily mineral, this is a really drinkable but complex Vinho Verde. It also has a mere 11% abv so that extra glass won't go amiss.

Pork belly

Slow cooked like this, pork belly can work with either whites or reds and my preference is for a rich white, like an Alsace Pinot Gris. However, I'd say nine out of ten people who ask for a recommendation for something like this are looking for a red so I'll go with a fabulous Spanish red that will easily do this great dish justice. **Huerta de Albala Barbazul, Cadiz 2010**, Andalucia's most ambitious quality wine project yet has produced this wine with a heady concoction of flavours in a seriously impressive wine. Made from a blend of Tintilla de Rota, Syrah and Merlot, this wine displays aromas of red berries, fig and aromatic herbs. On the palate Barbazul is warm, powerful and flavoursome with balanced acidity and impressive structure leading to a lovely long finish.

Tunisian orange cake

If the perfect match doesn't exist then this naturally sweet Moscatel and the Tunisian orange cake must be as close as it gets. The **Bodegas Bentomiz Arinyas Dulce, Malaga 2007** explodes with aromas of mandarin, clove, orange and jasmine blossom. On the palate it's perfectly balanced between sweet and fresh; being naturally sweet not fortified, it has a lightness of touch that marries perfectly with the moist orange cake.

p30

p80

p140

Essentials

There are certain simple stocks, sauces and dressings that are invaluable in the kitchen – they can be adapted to suit different recipes or tastes and can be used in various dishes. These are our favourites and most useful.

Basic white sauce

40g butter
40g plain flour
450ml milk

Notes: 450ml milk will make a sauce of a medium consistency. If you want a thick sauce, use 290ml and for a thin sauce use 570ml.

Melt the butter over a low heat in a saucepan, slowly add in the flour, stirring for 1-2 minutes until you have a smooth paste, or roux. Pour in approximately a fifth of the liquid you are using and boil without stirring. Using a balloon whisk, whisk until blended smoothly then gradually add the rest of the liquid to the desired consistency and season to taste.

At this point, the recipe can be adapted to make many different sauces. Here are a few:

Mornay sauce

Add 80-100g mature cheddar or a mix of Gruyère and Parmesan and stir in until melted but do not allow to boil. Great for cheesy leeks.

Béchamel

Grate in ½ tsp nutmeg, half a peeled onion with a couple of cloves in it, add 2 bay leaves and simmer gently for 10 minutes, adding more milk if too thick. Use in lasagne.

Parsley

Stir in 5 tbsp finely chopped parsley, 1 tbsp single cream and 1 tsp lemon juice.

Dressings

To make a basic vinaigrette, add 3 tbsp wine vinegar (red or white) with 8-9 tbsp olive oil to a jar and shake vigorously.

Use approximately a third vinegar to oil and this dressing can be adapted in lots of ways:

- Add balsamic vinegar and seasoning to make a balsamic vinaigrette.

- Add 1 tbsp honey and 1 tbsp wholegrain mustard for a honey and mustard alternative.

- Add garlic and freshly chopped oregano and leave for an hour to make Italian vinaigrette.

- Add 1tsp of Dijon mustard and 1 tsp dried mixed herbs of your choice to make a herb dressing. Stand for an hour to infuse flavours.

- Swap vinegar for lemon juice and add black pepper to make a lemon vinaigrette.

These dressings will keep for several weeks. If stored in the fridge, the oil may crystalise but will return to normal when brought back to room temperature.

Simple meat stock

(Makes 2 pints or 1 litre)

Bones of Sunday's roast

1 onion, quartered

1-2 carrots, chopped

1 stick of celery, chopped

5-6 peppercorns

1 bay leaf

1-2 sprigs thyme

Place all of the ingredients into a large pan and cover with cold water. Bring to the boil and skim the surface of the stock. Reduce the heat and simmer gently for 2-3 hours. Strain the stock into a jug and allow to cool, discarding the vegetables and herbs. Skim the surface again once cold.

Notes: Use within three days from fresh.

Simple vegetable stock

(Makes 2 pints or 1 litre)

1 tbsp olive oil

1 onion, chopped

1 carrot, chopped

½ leek, washed and sliced

3 cloves of garlic, peeled

½ tsp peppercorns

1 stick of celery, chopped

3 tomatoes, diced

3-4 stalks of parsley, torn

Heat the olive oil in a large pan and sweat the onion, carrot and leek for 2-3 minutes over a medium heat. Cover with cold water and increase the heat. Add the remaining vegetables, spices and herbs, stir and bring to the boil. Reduce the heat and cook gently for 15 minutes. Strain the stock into a jug and discard the vegetables.

Notes: Best used fresh.

Simple fish stock

(Makes 2 pints or 1 litre)

250g fish trimmings, washed

3 leeks, chopped

3 carrots, chopped

1 bulb of fennel, chopped

Handful of parsley, torn

175ml dry white wine

Place all the ingredients into a large pan and cover with cold water. Cook over a high heat until the liquid is simmering and skim any the surface with a spoon. Reduce the heat and simmer for no longer than 20 minutes, skimming again if necessary. Strain into a jug and discard trimmings, herbs and vegetables.

Notes: Use within two days from fresh.

All of these stocks can be frozen – just reduce by half, cool and pour into ice cube trays for handy cubes or freeze in batches to make it easier to portion for recipes. Use within one month.

Breadcrumbs

Place four slices of bread onto a baking tray and put into the oven at 180ºC. Bake for 5-10 minutes until the bread starts to dry out on the top side. Turn the bread over and return to the oven for a further 5 minutes.

Alternatively, leave slices of stale bread uncovered on a tray in a warm place for a couple of days until dried out. Place the dried bread in a food processor and blend until you have created fine/medium breadcrumbs. Store in an airtight jar or keep in the freezer.

How to steam rice

Many of the recipes in this book are served with rice. Light, fluffy steamed rice is much tastier than soggy boiled rice and it's actually really easy to do. The secret is to always use two parts water to one part rice and measure rice by volume in a measuring jug.

We're using 150g basmati rice, enough for two people.

Difficulty: ●●○○○
Preparation time: 5 mins
Cooking time: 30 mins

Serving: 2 portions

Storage: Keep covered in fridge for a day and reheat thoroughly once. Not suitable for freezing.

1. Rinse rice in a pan with a lid in cold water using your fingers to wash off the excess starch (you could use a colander). The water will turn milky to start with but should drain clear once the rice is washed.

2. Lay the back of your fingers on the rice and add water until your middle finger's knuckle is just covered.

3. Bring the pan to the boil for 5 or so minutes over a medium heat. Watch until bubbles start forming around the sides of the pan.

4. Turn the heat down to its lowest, cover with a tight fitting lid and leave for 15 minutes.

5. Turn the heat off completely and leave to stand for a further ten minutes. Do not lift the lid at any point or the rice won't steam properly!

6. The rice should have absorbed all the water and be soft. Using a fork or wooden spoon, fluff it up and then serve.

Conversion Tables

All recipes in the book are given in metric measurements. However, we've included some imperial conversions for those of you who choose to work in pounds and ounces. Conversions between the two can be inaccurate, for example 1 ounce equals 28g and multiples of 28 aren't easy to do maths with. Convention dictates that you use 25g to represent an ounce but if you want a more accurate recipe you will need a proper conversion. A quick way to measure small quantities of liquid is to use spoons instead of ml or fluid ounces. We've included all the options.

Weight

Ounces (oz)	Grams (g)	Exact
1	25	28
2	50	56
3	75	84
4	100	112
5	125	140
6	150	168
7	175	196
8	200	224
9	225	252
10	250	280
11	275	308
12	300	336
13	325	364
14	350	392
15	375	420
16/1lb	400	448

Volume

Imperial	ml	Spoons
	5	1 teaspoon (tsp)
	10	1 dessertspoon
½ fluid ounce	15	1 tablespoon (tbsp)
1fl oz	30	
2fl oz	60	
5 (¼ pint)	150	
10 (½ pint)	300	
15 (¾ pint)	450	
1 pint	600	
1 ¼ pint	750	
1 ¾ pint	1 litre	

Oven temperatures

Gas	Celsius (°C)	Fahrenheit (°F)
1	140	284
2	150	302
3	160	320
4	180	374
5	190	392
6	200	410
7	210	428
8	220	446
9	240	464

The temperatures given in the book are for fan assisted ovens. For fanless ovens the general rule is to increase the temperature by 20°C. If in doubt, consult the manufacturer's guidelines for suitable cooking temperatures with your oven.

WI Wisdom

At one of our monthly meetings we asked members to give us their top tips for the home. Whether it's dealing with leftovers or better enjoying a G&T, we've got it here!

General kitchen tips

Use lemon juice to reduce the spiciness of dishes. Also works if you have chilli burn on your skin. The acid neutralises the strong alkaline of the chilli.

To prevent hands from getting a garlic odour or chilli burn, rub skin with a little oil beforehand. It acts as a barrier and makes it easier to wash off with soap.

Chopping chillies, garlic and ginger for curries – rather than do this by hand, put pieces of these in a mini blender and whizz them up together. It is quick and easy and means you don't rub your eyes after chopping chilli!

Light a candle whilst cooking fish to eliminate fish smell.

Use a potato ricer to make perfect mashed potatoes.

Cut a lemon or lime into 8 parts and freeze to put in gin and tonic instead of ice.

If you forget to soften butter, fill a glass with very hot water from the tap. Tip out the water and dry quickly, then place the warm glass over the amount of butter that you need. The butter will soften very quickly (about a minute).

Keep an aloe vera plant in the kitchen – the juice in the leaves is really good for minor burns.

Keep bananas away from other fruit unless you want it to ripen – bananas give off ethylene gas which will ripen all fruits and vegetables.

Jacket potatoes will cook a lot quicker if you put two skewers through them, crossing in the middle.

To crack an egg without the shell coming out with it – knock the egg gently on a flat surface rather than a sharp edge. If you do get a bit of shell in the broken egg, then use another, larger, bit of the shell to fish it out – the fragment will be attracted to the big piece. Much easier than trying to fish it out with your fingers!

Dust raisins, berries or chocolate chips with flour to stop them sinking in cakes mixes.

If you don't have a rolling pin use an empty bottle!

What to do with leftover...

Silken tofu
Whizz up in a food processor with 2 ripe bananas and a couple of teaspoons of cocoa powder. Makes a nutritious pudding for kids – who think it's pure chocolate!

Egg whites
Freeze them. They are actually better for making meringues as freezing them dries them out and breaks down the protein so they inflate better.

Dips/pesto
Use to top bruschetta or use in potato salad as an alternative to mayonnaise.

Herbs
Whizz up with oil to make herb oil or chop and put into ice cube trays with a little water. Add to soups etc, or use frozen mint in mint tea.

Wine
Freeze in ice cube trays and thaw and use in sauces when a recipe requires it. Don't let kids mistake frozen red wine for blackcurrant!

Salmon
Make fishcakes. If you use a jacket potato in the fishcakes then you can use the potato skins up by sprinkling with olive oil and cooking in the oven.

Bread
An alternative way to make bread crumbs is by blitzing the bread in a food processor, then spreading it out on a baking sheet or baking paper. Leave overnight to dry out and then store in an airtight jar. Or put in the freezer. It'll keep for months!

Vanilla pod
If you use a whole vanilla pod (eg to make custard), rinse and dry it after use and then put in an airtight container with caster sugar. Hey presto, vanilla sugar.

Avocado
To stop cut avocados from turning brown, refrigerate them flesh side down in a bowl of water into which you have squeezed some lemon juice.

Parmesan rinds
Keep them in the fridge and throw them into soups for a deeper flavour.

Bones
Keep old chicken carcasses or joint bones in bags and put in the freezer. Use them to make stock.

Bananas
If bananas are black, spotty and on the verge of turning from ripe to rotten, put them in the freezer so you can keep them on hand for making banana loaf.

Put a couple of grains of rice in your salt to stop it sticking together.

Save time chopping herbs and keep them all contained by cutting them up in a pint glass with scissors.

Use a balloon whisk (or a hand blender) for getting lumps out of gravy/sauces.

If you're freezing berries spread them out on a baking tray and freeze before tipping into a bag. This stops them from sticking together.

You can tell if a pineapple is ripe by seeing if a leaf pulls out easily.

Natural cleaning methods

Washing machines – periodically I run my washing machine at 90°C with nothing in it. This was recommended to me by a washing machine repair man who said it is a good way of prolonging the life of a washing machine and keeping it clean. Also stops mould and bacteria building up.

Sprinkle bicarbonate of soda into a stainless steel sink and add a bit of water to allow the bicarbonate to turn into a paste. Then use a cloth to wipe clean and rinse.

Use lemon juice to remove garlic odour from hands.

After a roast, add a bowl of boiling water to the oven. This helps get rid of fat, then you can just wipe clean.

To clean a microwave put a small bowl of water with a slice of lemon in and boil for two minutes. Leave for a further three minutes and then open and wipe clean.

To clean a dishwasher, fill a plastic cup about two thirds full with vinegar and put in bottom shelf of dishwasher. Put dishwasher on for a short wash. At end of cycle, pour away the vinegar. This is a safe effective way to keep your dishwasher clean.

Thank you

This book represents the culmination of an idea I had whilst riding my bike home from work one day. It's taken a lot of hard work from a small group of individuals, and was born from a shared love of Gloucester Road and a passion for food. There are several groups and individuals I'd like to thank, without whom the book simply wouldn't have been possible.

The first big thank you, for obvious reasons, goes to the project team. From the start you were enthusiastic and raring to go, and your support and positivity has continued throughout the project. It's amazing what a small group of people can do in less than a year, in addition to work and home commitments and without the motivation of pay! The project has taken up more time than we ever expected, but I hope you will agree that it was worth it. The book that you have produced is something to be proud of; a book which reflects your skills, expertise, professionalism and good taste!

A huge thank you to the wider Gloucester Road WI members too, your recipes and wisdom will inspire others to get cooking and we feel honoured that you've given us access to recipes that mean so much to you.

A massive thank you to all the businesses that have contributed to this cookbook. Without your support this book wouldn't exist. Your enthusiasm has been fantastic, and your community spirit uplifting. Thank you for trusting in our idea and for giving us the opportunity to produce such a special book.

And finally, I'd also like to say a big thank you to the Gloucester Rd WI committee who gave us the green light to start the project in late 2012. Your support has been invaluable.

Katie

Katie Skuse,
Project leader
and member of
Gloucester Rd WI

From top: Katie Skuse; testing, prepping and photography at Danielle's house; helpers Kit and Betsy the dog; a cookbook meeting under way!

The project team

Danielle Coombs
Chef and food consultant

Danielle is a freelance chef and runs Bishopston Supper Club.

www.restingchef.wordpress.com

@RestingChef
@BishopstonSC

Sarah Newman
Publisher

Thanks to Sarah for sorting out the publishing element when she should have been working!

www.iamsarahnewman.tumblr.com

Kate Debley
Assistant chef and testing

Kate headed up the testing and handed over her home to photography on several occasions.

Claire-Louise Partridge
Project manager

CLP has a love of spreadsheets and kept us all in line and updated throughout the project.

Michaela Parker
Writing and editing

Michaela is a freelance features writer, journalist and sub-editor who can always be found with a notebook and a dictaphone to hand.

www.michaelaparker.co.uk

@Michaela_writer

India Rabey
Design and photography

India is a freelance design consultant and graphic designer as well as the founder and current president of Gloucester Rd WI.

www.indiarabey.co.uk

India Rabey Graphic Design

@IndiaRabey

Further big thanks go to:

Judy Gowenlock for her hard work signing up businesses, writing the introduction to Gloucester Road and her excellent local knowledge · **Kirstie** for keeping an eye on the money side of things and also helping to sign up businesses · **Amanda Clarke** for proof reading and helping out at the fundraising events. · **Rima Bhattacharya** for helping at the fundraising events and her enthusiasm during long meetings.

Directory

Here's the definitive list of all the businesses showcased in the cookbook. Listed in numerical order along Gloucester Road.

The Prince of Wales

Welcoming pub with a large range of ales, home cooked food and a cosy covered courtyard at rear. Dog friendly.

5 Gloucester Rd, Bristol BS7 8AA
0117 924 5552
info@powbristol.co.uk
www.powbristol.co.uk

Harvest

Independent co-operative retailer specialising in vegetarian and vegan foods. Part of Essential Trading Co-operative in Bristol.

11 Gloucester Rd, Bristol BS7 8AA
0117 942 5997
info@harvest-bristol.coop
www.harvest-bristol.coop

Tart

A good old-fashioned tea room with a remarkable selection of cakes and light meals popular with everyone.

16 The Promenade, Gloucester Rd, Bristol BS7 8AE
0117 924 7628
Tart Cafe and Foodstore
@Lovelytart1
www.lovelytart.com

The Gallimaufry

Home cooking and curios bar as it says above the door! A wide range of drinks and a seasonally changing menu.

26 The Promenade, Gloucester Rd, Bristol BS7 8AE
0117 942 7319
info@thegallimaufry.co.uk
TheGallimaufryBristol
@TheGalliBristol
www.thegallimaufry.co.uk

Bubalu

Bristol's only fitness café. Try out the spinning class then cool down with a smoothie in the café.

79/81 Gloucester Rd, Bristol BS7 8AS
0117 924 5381
bristol@bubalu.co.uk
BubaluBristol
@bubalubristol
www.bubalu.co.uk

Scrumptiously Sweet

A truly traditional sweet shop. Buy all manner of sugary delights, pre-packed or by weight, and even pick up some cake tins and icing materials.

83 Gloucester Rd, Bristol BS7 8AS
07919 526 582
enquiries@scrumptiouslysweet.co.uk
Scrumptiously Sweet
@s_sweetbs7
www.scrumptiouslysweet.co.uk

Playfull Toys

A lovely little toy shop where play is positively encouraged! A large selection of craft materials and books to browse as well.

87 Gloucester Rd, Bristol BS7 8AS
playfullkp@hotmail.com
0117 944 6767
Playfull Toyshop

Grape and Grind

Learn your claret from your beaujolais at Gloucester Road's only independent wine merchant. Join the Wine Club.

101 Gloucester Rd, Bristol BS7 8AT
0117 924 8718
info@grapeandgrind.co.uk
Grape & Grind
@grapegrind
www.grapeandgrind.co.uk

102 Cookery School

Nailsea Electrical's purpose-built cookery school in a converted church. Learn all manner of culinary skills from the experts.

102 Gloucester Rd, Bristol BS7 8BN
0117 244 0047
admin@102cookeryschool.co.uk
102cookeryschool
@102Cookery
www.102cookeryschool.co.uk

The Family Practice

Combining osteopathy and complementary therapies to give a wholly individual healthcare and treatment strategy.

116 Gloucester Rd, Bristol BS7 8NL
0117 944 6968
www.thefamilypractice.tv

Bristanbul

Bristol's only Turkish bakery/patisserie. Freshly made baklava and occasional cakes. Or why not enjoy a nice cup of Turkish coffee with a fresh slice of cake inside and feel like you're really there?

137 Gloucester Rd, Bristol BS7 8AX
0117 924 0003
Bristanbul Patisserie
www.bristanbul.co.uk

The Fish Shop

Freshly delivered fish from Devon and Cornwall. All products ethically sourced and of the highest quality available.

143 Gloucester Rd, Bristol BS7 8BA
0117 924 1988 / 07821 699 065
info@lovethefishshop.co.uk
lovethefishshop
@lovethefishshop
www.lovethefishshop.com

Gardner's Patch

A proper family-run grocers in the heart of Bishopston. Lots of local and seasonal produce as well as some of the more exotic.

159 Gloucester Rd, Bristol BS7 8BA
0117 923 2367
@GardnersPatch
www.gardnerspatch.co.uk

Dave Giles

Traditional family butcher. Homemade sausages and burgers a speciality. Also sells dairy products and preserves.

170 Gloucester Rd, Bristol BS7 8NU
0117 942 5667
davethebutcher58@hotmail.com

Atomic Burger

For the best burgers, pulled pork and milkshakes for miles around. Try the Fallout Challenge, if you dare!

189 Gloucester Rd, Bristol BS7 8BG
0117 942 8600
bristol@atomicburger.co.uk
Atomic burger
@atomicburgers
www.atomicburger.co.uk

Delmonico

Modern British restaurant with freshly prepared, locally sourced dishes and excellent coffee.

217A Gloucester Rd, Bristol BS7 8NN
0117 944 5673
info@delmonico.co.uk
www.delmonico.co.uk

Zazu's Kitchen

Breakfast, lunch and dinner are served in this quirky, friendly, neighbourhood restaurant with a focus on seasonal produce.

225 Gloucester Rd, Bristol BS7 8NR
0117 944 5500
info@zazuskitchen.co.uk
@ZazusKitchen225
www.zazuskitchen.co.uk

Joe's Bakery

Bakery selling everything from croissants to cakes and flour to granary loaves. Joe's Express next door sells sandwiches and lunches to go.

240–242 Gloucester Rd, Bristol BS7 8NZ
0117 975 5551
@JaneJoesBakery
www.joesbakery.co.uk

Pearce's Hardware

Truly a shop that sells everything! From garden rakes to door handles and from dish cloths to paint. If you need it for the home, they probably have it!

293 Gloucester Rd, Bristol BS7 8PE
0117 924 5787

Kookoo Cafe

Right at the top of Gloucester Road is this cosy Persian restaurant. Open in the evenings for dinners. BYO.

429 Gloucester Rd, Bristol BS7 8TZ
0117 951 6661
kookoocafebristol@gmail.com
f KookoocafeBristol

Sponsors

Bishopston Matters

Started in 2007 as a community magazine for Bishopston, St Andrews, Horfield and Ashley Down, what was once a 28-page black and white publication has grown into an 80-page full colour affair that is delivered to over 10,500 homes per quarter.

Editor/photographer/saleswoman extraordinaire Kerry Allen is dedicated to providing local residents with community news and events from a planning and involvement perspective, and the magazine's success is owed to each of the traders and individuals that feature within it.

Working closely with the traders of Gloucester Road, Kerry produces a magazine that works for everyone and she is always happy to hear from new groups and individuals who would like to get in touch.

0117 3494483 / 07881 924059
kerry@bishopstonmatters.co.uk
@bishmatters
www.bishopstonmatters.co.uk

Fig

Fig is a treasure trove of trinkets, art and jewellery, all lovingly created by a group of six local artists and craftspeople who began working together in 2009. Originally started as a co-operative and workplace from which they could each sell their wares, the space has now been fully opened up as a shop and gallery space.

Offering up the bespoke to the truly unique, Fig sells everything from jewellery to glassware, textiles, cards and t-shirts and as the artists are right there, many of the products on offer can be personalised for that all important gift.

Huge fans of the diversity that Gloucester Road has to offer, Fig fits in perfectly to the independent high street.

206 Gloucester Rd, Bristol BS7 8NU
0117 924 4898
figshop@btconnect.com
www.figshop.co.uk

FREE!
Box of six premium cupcakes
from Joe's Bakery

Expires 31.08.14. Pre-orders only with three working days' notice. Offer limited to one box per book. Offers can be redeemed by phoning the order through on 0117 9755551 or coming into the shop. Hand in voucher on collection. Joe's Bakery, 240-242 Gloucester Rd, Bristol BS7 8NZ.

20% off
Vouchers, classes or bookings
at 102 Cookery School

Expires 31.07.14. 20% off customer's first purchase on all gift vouchers, hands on classes, group bookings and corporate events. Voucher can be redeemed once only. Hand in voucher on arrival. Call the school or email to redeem voucher. 102 Gloucester Rd, Bristol BS7 8BN.

FREE!
Dessert at Delmonico

Expires 31.07.14 (excluding December 2013). A free dessert when dining from our two course early evening menu. This menu is valid Monday to Friday 12-7.30pm and Saturday 12-7pm. Present voucher at time of ordering. Voucher can be redeemed once only. 217A Gloucester Rd, Bristol BS7 8NN.

20% off
Meal & drinks
at The Prince of Wales

Expires 30.11.14. 20% off a meal and drinks for up to four people. Customers to notify staff on arrival with presentation of voucher in order to set up a tab. Voucher can be redeemed once only. 5 Gloucester Rd, Bristol BS7 8AA.

FREE!
Bottle of wine
at The Gallimaufry

Free bottle of house wine for À La Carte restaurant bookings for two or more people, Mon-Fri only. Expires 31.01.14 (excluding December 2013). Voucher can be redeemed once only. Present voucher to staff on arrival. 26 The Promenade, Gloucester Rd, Bristol BS7 8AE.

15% off
at Fig

Expires 15.10.14. 15% off any purchase at Fig in a single transaction on presentation of voucher. Voucher can be redeemed once only. 206 Gloucester Rd, Bristol BS7 8NU.

10% off
first advert & free article on website
in Bishopston Matters

Expires 31.12.14. Voucher can be redeemed once only. 10% discount to any business for first advertisement placed in the magazine and a free article (provided by them) on the front page of the website. Email kerry@bishopstonmatters.co.uk or call 07881 924 059.

The
Gloucester
Road
**Cook
book**

The
Gloucester
Road
**Cook
book**

The
Gloucester
Road
**Cook
book**

The
Gloucester
Road
**Cook
book**

The
Gloucester
Road
**Cook
book**

The
Gloucester
Road
**Cook
book**

The
Gloucester
Road
Cookbook

Index